K. SATYANARAYANA is associate professc
tural Studies, English and Foreign Lang
derabad. Active in the student movement during the 1990s, ne was
founder-general secretary of Kula Nirmoolana Porata Samiti (Forum
for Caste Annihilation). He also edited the little magazine *Kulanir-moolana*. His research interests are in the field of dalit studies and literary history. He is co-editor of *No Alphabet in Sight* and *Steel Nibs are Sprouting*, two comprehensive anthologies of dalit writing from South India.

SUSIE THARU is professor in the Department of Cultural Studies, EFLU, and a founder member of Anveshi, Research Centre for Women's Studies, Hyderabad. She is the author of several influential papers on literary and cultural theory and history. She has been active in the Indian women's movement and is a member of the Subaltern Studies Collective. Tharu is co-editor of the two-volume anthology *Women Writing in India*, as well as *No Alphabet in Sight* and *Steel Nibs are Sprouting*.

navayana

THE EXERCISE OF
FREEDOM

AN INTRODUCTION TO DALIT WRITING

Edited and Introduced by
**K. SATYANARAYANA
AND SUSIE THARU**

The Exercise of Freedom: An Introduction to Dalit Writing
First published by Navayana Publishing Pvt Ltd, 2013

Prescribed as core text for the Complementary Course on Dalit
Writing, Semesters 1 to 4, B.A. English Language and Literature,
University of Kerala

Pages 182–83 are an extension of the copyright page
© Introduction and selection, K. Satyanarayana and Susie Tharu

ISBN 9788189059613

Database right, Navayana Publishing Pvt Ltd

Navayana Publishing Pvt Ltd
155 2nd Floor, Shahpur Jat
New Delhi 110049
Phone: 91-11-26494795
navayana.org

Typeset in Dante at Navayana

Printed and bound by Sanjiv Palliwal, New Delhi

Subscribe to updates at navayana.org/subscribe
Follow on facebook.com/Navayana

CONTENTS

MODULE III

I

MODULE IV

I

DALIT WRITING: AN INTRODUCTION

K. SATYANARAYANA AND SUSIE THARU

What is dalit writing and how do we approach it? Is it simply a new literary trend? If so, we would regard it as a body of writing that expands the field of literature by bringing a new social reality into literary discussion. The next steps would be to identify the best works, create a canon of dalit literature and promote the critical appreciation of new poetry, autobiography, short stories and other literary forms. Such an approach, however, would miss important dimensions of the historical rise of dalit critical and creative writing and its actual current significance.

Dalit literature does not grow out of literary discussion or the practice of writers. It is a social movement invested in the battle against injustice and driven by the hope of freedom, not simply a *literary* trend or a formal development. This literature encompasses diverse forms of intellectual and creative work by those who, as untouchables, are victims of economic, social and cultural inequality. Using the term 'dalit writing' helps us emphasize the relation with the social and political concerns of dalit movements. There are other aspects of dalit writing that we need to consider carefully.

Indian or Hindu literature?

In an important essay on dalit literature, the Marathi dalit critic and writer, Baburao Bagul, argues that "the established literature of India is Hindu literature"[1] and that the 'lowest' castes are excluded in Indian literature because of its Hindu character. He explains: "Writers who have internalised the Hindu value-structure find it impossible to accept heroes, themes and thoughts derived from the philosophies of Phule and Ambedkar" (*PB*, 285). Bagul and other dalit critics also

---

[1] Arjun Dangle, ed., *Poisoned Bread: Translations from Modern Marathi Dalit Literature* (Hyderabad: Orient Longman, 1992), 289.

analyze the reasons for the exclusion and biased representation of dalits and 'lower castes' in Indian literatures.[2] What is more, they question the very basis on which the category of Indian literature is developed. These critics and thinkers re-read Indian nationalist history and literature. They also reinterpret colonial rule and revisit the Gandhi–Ambedkar dialogue. Their critical engagement enables them to show that Indian literature is elite, Hindu and upper caste. Dalit literature, they demonstrate, represents a new thinking and a new point of view. It poses the question of the representation of dalit and lower caste life ('heroes, themes and thoughts' from dalit society) as a critical public issue.

It is important to understand the reasons for what many writers have called the 'chasm' between dalit literature and what went before it. The canons of modern Indian literatures as well as that of Indian writing in English are constituted of works and critical attitudes that are shaped by an anticolonial nationalism. Although history books are written as though this was the only form of nationalism that existed, anticolonial nationalism is actually Congress nationalism, and more specifically, Gandhian nationalism. In such nationalist thinking, the entire story of the struggle for freedom is told as one of opposition between the colonizer and colonized. Indian literature is a literature in which the colonized reply or 'write back' to the authority of Empire.

The principal themes of this Indian literature are anticolonial consciousness, the tensions between tradition and modernity, the Indian struggle for independence, the glory of Indian civilization and so on. It should not surprise us that such literature evades addressing the internal contradictions and complexities in the life of the colonized. When, as in some early writing, such issues are raised, they are represented as problems that can be solved by the ruling elite. The canonical writers of Indian literatures generally did not discuss caste, class, gender and other inequalities in a radical way. These 'internal' problems, it was believed, would divide Indians. They portrayed peas-

---

[2] We do not endorse the hierarchy implied in the use of 'lower' and 'upper' castes. We retain the popular usage because it carries the stamp and the memory of power and history. Neither can be displaced in a verbal gesture.

ants, workers and adivasis—all integrated into the Gandhian national movement. In other words, the Gandhian mobilization of all sections of Indians to present a united force to challenge British rule obscured many questions of inequalities amongst Indians, most importantly, the questions of freedom from slavery and untouchability. Even novelists who attempted to represent dalit and lower caste life do not escape the ideological hold of Gandhian thinking on their representation of dalits. Unnava Lakshmi Narayana's *Malapalli* (1922), in Telugu, and Mulk Raj Anand's *Untouchable* (1935), in English, and several other Indian language novels can be cited as examples of this trend. In many of the canonical texts of Indian literature, Gandhi appears as a symbol, and sometimes even as a character. Such is the presence of Gandhian nationalism in Indian literatures.

Such exclusion of dalit and lower caste questions cannot be viewed in isolation from the nationalist process through which the canons of Indian literatures were formed. Dalit critics have argued that despite its seeming concern with untouchability, Gandhian nationalism actually suppressed important questions that were articulated by Dr B.R. Ambedkar (1891–1956) and other dalit leaders (whom we discuss later). For example, Ambedkar had argued that treating as equal those who are not equal, only increased inequality. Dalits, he said, had special needs. So he asked that they be recognized as a minority, requiring special attention in Indian society. This demand was quickly dismissed as anti-national and, by implication, pro-British. In sum, Gandhi gave priority to anticolonial political struggle which, he said, would solve all other problems, while Ambedkar argued that social equality among the Indians was as important as independence.

Babasaheb Ambedkar

However, in a surprisingly short time these key tensions and debates, and in fact the very memory of Ambedkar and the significance of his thought were suppressed and erased from mainstream Indian history. Historians paid little attention to these issues and school textbooks did not mention him. The voluminous writings of this important Indian thinker were not available in libraries or bookshops. The Ambedkarian strand of history was forgotten. Only in the late 1960s and 1970s,

Marathi (the Dalit Panthers) and Kannada (in the Dalit Sangharsh Samiti) dalit thinkers and writers began turning back to Ambedkar. The fuller re-establishment of Ambedkar as a national icon and an inspiration for Indian democracy happens only in the 1990s. It is during that decade that Ambedkar was resurrected as a dalit leader, constitutionalist and major Indian intellectual. Alert to these developments the Indian government decided, several years after his death, to award him the Bharat Ratna, in 1990. His birth centenary celebration in 1991 is a turning point in the history of contemporary dalit movements. When Ambedkar and his ideas (statues, writings, discussions and public meetings) resurfaced in the public domain a series of new questions came up for discussion. The dalit perspective on colonialism and Ambedkar's critique of Gandhian nationalism are two such questions.

In mainstream nationalist thought only the exploitative and oppressive aspect of colonialism, and the fact that it involved foreign rule, were considered significant. This nationalism interpreted colonialism only as economic and political domination. But colonialism was also a context in which a great deal of social and cultural change took place. Colonial presence was not limited to the British army and administration. It also involved missionary activity, which included the setting up of educational institutions and hospitals as well as conversions, reform of many social practices, the emergence of public spaces that were accessible to all, the introduction of modern life and the rule of law. All these were part of what came about as a result of colonial rule. The marginalized and culturally stigmatized sections of Indian society did not oppose colonialism or think of it only as anti-Indian rule. They adopted a strategic view of colonialism as a moment of structural reorganization of Indian society. They invoked the normative ideas of equality and modernity, made use of colonial educational institutions, converted to Christianity and organized their communities as religious and social pressure groups. But the nationalists who advocated anticolonialism as the primary task described the dalit religious and social movements as sectarian and pro-British. The ideas of Ambedkar and other anti-caste thinkers such as Ayyankali, Iyothee Thass, Swami Achhutanand and Kusuma Dharmanna among others were buried in this nationalist view.

When we return like this to the history of the independence movement and examine the views of leaders like Ambedkar who stood outside the Congress mainstream, alternative perspectives of independence and freedom emerge. For example, Gandhi described untouchables as 'harijan.' The term 'harijan' literally means children of God. Ambedkar rejected this name for being Hindu, and for being patronizing and derogatory. Gandhi argued that the untouchables are an inseparable part of Hindu society. He denied a separate identity to untouchables and opposed separate electorates and other claims based on untouchable identity. Gandhi described the varna order as an ideal system of ancient India and wanted it to continue. The only aspect of it that he opposed was untouchability, which he looked at as 'inhuman' and 'a blot' on Hinduism, a religion he upheld. Ambedkar disagreed with Gandhi and gave a call for the annihilation of caste. For Ambedkar, caste as a system and as a practice is undemocratic. It does not allow for interaction, communication, unity or societal mobility of people. Caste is sanctified by Hinduism. What is more, Hinduism as a religion sanctions graded inequality, divine retribution, divine will and violence. Therefore, Ambedkar contended, there is no democracy and equality possible in Hinduism.

Ambedkar consciously shaped a distinct identity for dalits and institutionalized their constitutional rights. He referred to the untouchables as 'depressed classes', 'scheduled castes' and also as 'dalits' depending on the context. The term 'dalit' was popularized by the Dalit Panthers. Today it is the most favoured mode of referring to this group. 'Dalit' literally means 'crushed down'. It is a name that untouchables have given themselves. Other demeaning appellations—chandala, bhangi, panchama, etc—are given by the dominant castes, but dalit is an identity of dignity and self-assertion. Though the term was initially used to refer to all the oppressed including untouchables (such as in the Dalit Panthers' Manifesto), it later acquired the meaning it now has, as an identity of the untouchable castes. In other words, 'dalit' is a democratic identity of the socially oppressed untouchable caste groups.

The Beginnings

The beginnings of dalit literature are traced back to Ambedkar's struggles for dalit emancipation in the early twentieth century. Ambedkar pioneers what we think of today as dalit writing. Marathi dalit critics cite the legacy of Buddha (sixth century BCE), Cokhamela, the fourteenth century bhakti saint, Mahatma Jotiba Phule (1828–90) and Prof S.M. Mate (1886–1957) as the originators of the anti-caste movements and literatures in the Marathi-speaking region. Among the many other pioneering dalit figures that recent research has uncovered are Iyothee Thass (1845–1914), Tamil scholar and publisher; Kusuma Dharmanna (1894–1948) and Bhagya Reddy Varma (1845–1939), Telugu reformers and social thinkers; Ayyankali (1863–1941), Malayali political leader; and Poykayil Yohannan (1878–1939), Malayali visionary and religious leader.

Dalit historians trace the history of the term 'dalit literature' to the first Dalit Literary Conference in 1958. Anna Bhau Sathe, a prominent Marathi writer, delivered the inaugural speech. The conference discussed dalit literature and passed the following resolution among others: "that the literature written by the dalits and that written by others about the dalits in Marathi be accepted as a separate entity known as 'dalit literature' and realizing its cultural importance, universities and literary organizations should give it its proper place" (*PB*, 242).[3]

Baburao Bagul's 1963 collection of short stories, *Jevha Mi Jaat Chorli Hoti* (When I Concealed my Caste), was hailed as 'the epic of dalits'. These brilliant stories gave dalits the strength to face the painful and humiliating experiences of their lives. Not only that, it inspired them to shape these experiences creatively. The collection opened up new formal and thematic ground and gave dalit literary thinking a huge momentum. Anna Bhau Sathe, whose story of the epic struggle to survive and remain human, "Gold from the Grave",

---

[3] This early formulation was revised by Sharan Kumar Limbale thus: "By dalit literature I mean writing about dalits by dalit writers with a dalit consciousness." This would be the stand that is broadly accepted today. See *Towards an Aesthetic of Dalit Literature: History, Controversies and Considerations*, trans. Alok Mukherjee (Hyderabad: Orient Longman, 2004), 19. Marathi publication, 1996.

is presented in this collection, was also writing around this time. The real flowering of dalit writing, however, begins in the 1970s when a number of younger poets and short story writers emerged. Namdeo Dhasal, Arjun Dangle and J.V. Pawar took the initiative of establishing a new militant dalit organization called Dalit Panthers in Bombay in 1972.

The "Dalit Panthers' Manifesto" (1973), reprinted here, returns to the Gandhi–Ambedkar debate and brings Ambedkar into the mainstream of public discourse. The Panthers criticized Gandhi for preserving 'class rule' and endorsed Ambedkar's criticism of Gandhi. They wrote: "Merely to preserve the unity of the independence struggle, he flirted with problems of dalits, of untouchability and of the people. And that is why Babasaheb Ambedkar called him, time and again, 'the enemy of the people, the villain of the nation'."

Leading Dalit Panthers were all writers. They brought in a new point of view, a new thinking and a language that left Marathi literature shaken and transformed. They began to describe the reality of dalit life with an insight that came from those who belonged to the community and had first-hand experience of dalit life. These descriptions of slavery and oppression, as well as the open and hidden forms of caste discrimination in the contemporary world, were unlike anything that had been written before. Their claims to freedom, dignity, self-respect and equality gave new meaning to these primary concepts of democratic life. Marathi dalit literature had created history in the 1970s and 1980s. Several collections of poems, short stories, autobiographical extracts, essays and speeches have been published in the last thirty years. A sample of these in English translation appeared in 1992 in what is now a classic, *Poisoned Bread: Translations from Modern Marathi Dalit Literature*. The Panthers were an important influence on the Dalit Sangharsha Samiti (DSS) which overturned the assumptions of the Kannada literary and social world in the 1970s.[4] Key figures in

---

[4] For an account of the 'Boosa' episode that precipitated the formation of the DSS in Karnataka, and the famous struggles around the atrocities in Karamchedu that gave rise to the dalit movement in Andhra Pradesh, see K. Satyanarayana and Susie Tharu, *From those Stubs, Steel Nibs are Sprouting* (New Delhi: HarperCollins, 2013), 2–24.

the DSS were the critic B. Krishnappa, the scholar and poet Siddalingaiah, and the novelist Devanoora Mahadeva, all of whom have been represented in this collection.

With the rise of autonomous dalit movements in South India in the 1970s and after, dalit literature made its presence felt in Karnataka, Andhra Pradesh, Tamil Nadu and Kerala. While Kannada dalit writing was inspired and shaped by Lohiaite as well as Ambedkarite ideas, Telugu, Tamil and Malayalam dalit literature of the 1990s drew on the icon and ideologue, Ambedkar. A selection of these writings has been translated and published in two volumes: *No Alphabet in Sight* (2011) and *Steel Nibs are Sprouting* (2013).

Dalit writing is now a pan-Indian phenomenon with the rise of dalit writing in Hindi and other Indian languages post 1990s. The critical perspective of this new writing, what we think of today as a *dalit* perspective, has shifted away from the old approach of viewing caste as a problem of the past (Hinduism, nationalism, history) to that of viewing caste as an issue of present times. It also moves from viewing caste as a problem that lower castes face to viewing caste as an issue that affects the whole of society. Questions such as modernity, contemporary forms of caste, conversion, identity and discrimination are central to dalit writing now. The ideological legacies, both of Marxism and the Dravidian movement are critically examined in this writing. We discuss some themes of this new writing in the next section.

1970s and After: Freedom, Dignity, Self-Respect

A whole new set of writings *by* dalits begins to appear in the 1970s. These writings criticized and rejected ideas of reform and uplift. They showed that although caste and class are related, caste cannot be reduced to class. They demonstrated that the non-brahmin consolidation of the Dravidian movement continues to exclude dalits. They began to describe the reality of dalit life with insights that came from those who belonged to the community and had first-hand experience of dalit life. Their descriptions of slavery, oppression, the struggle for survival, love, hate, humiliation and the wretchedness of dalit life were unlike anything that had been written before. It becomes clear that caste is not simply a prejudice, but a form of power and of economic, social and cultural capital in the contemporary world. In this context, dalit aspirations for freedom, dignity, self respect and equality infuse these primary concepts of democratic life with fresh concrete and grounded meanings. The arrival of the 'dalit' is exuberantly announced in a number of writings. In this book you will encounter two of them: the "Dalit Panthers' Manifesto" and Siddalingaiah's poem, "The Dalits are Here". With this shift, new settings, new themes, new arguments and new attitudes began to appear in the literature. We discuss some of them below.

Caste in Contemporary Life

The idea that caste discrimination and violence is found only in traditional societies, that it is a residue of tradition, or that the practice was to be found only among Hindus, were shown to be mistaken. Dalit writers demonstrated that humiliation, rejection and exclusion based on caste were common practice in contemporary India. In fact caste discrimination takes on new forms in modern life. Its workings are comparable to the workings of race and gender discrimination.

In Ajay Navaria's "New Custom", for instance, the narrator, who is also the central character, is educated and makes a decent living. He has money, is carefully dressed, and has professional status. His scientific awareness of hygiene, his discomfort with the representation of women as sex objects, his concern with issues of equality and dignity make him, in fact, more modern and enlightened than those around him. All the same, in the eyes of the man who runs the teashop and of others around him, the protagonist is only an untouchable. The story also directs our attention to the constant everyday pressure that requires a dalit who moves into the upper caste world to make sure he cannot be seen as 'unclean' or primitive. We might think about all this as a new kind of violence—the everyday, continuous, psychological violence of social and cultural power. The word custom suggests a practice that has been followed for a long time. The reader may find it interesting to think of the different senses in which the apparently contradictory phrase 'new custom' is used here. The narrator's critical self-consciousness is a special touch. In the midst of the adventure which involves his being 'exposed' as an untouchable, is a sub-plot in which he catches himself feeling happy at being mistaken for an upper caste person. Despite being against caste, personally and politically, the hold of caste is so subtle and pervasive, the writer suggests, that even such a person has not managed to escape it.

Caste may no longer be called caste, but it is everywhere. It goes by other names and is practised by everyone. One of the most important contributions of the new dalit writing is its analysis of such everyday and subtle forms of power.

S. Joseph's poem "Identity Card" is set in a college.[5] In this modern institution where other traditional beliefs have no place, boy and girl meet, share meals, exchange books, discuss poetry and politics, dream of freedom. They both exude the joy and openness of youth. All is fine—until she sees his identity card with evidence of his caste visible in the stipend payments entered there in red. She feels cheated; leaves. The irony here is that the very thing (his identity card) that gives him access to education and as a result freedom from his traditional role is also what exposes and, in fact, excludes him. You may think you have loosened the tentacles of caste, but it finds another way of keeping you in its clutch. Rekharaj's essay, "Rajani's suicide" proceeds step by step to implicate banks, educational establishments, the press and the government in this young student's death. In an important poem, not in this collection, M. Satish Chander probes the demoralization that results from failure—an all too common experience for dalit students in a system set up and run by upper castes, with the success of upper castes in mind. He traces the lineage of the pedagogic attitude that cannot accept dalit success back to Dronacharya who cut off Eklavya's thumb.[6]

The two essays from "Dalit Diary", Chandra Bhan Prasad's pathbreaking column in *The Pioneer*, reveal a new understanding of untouchability. It is now shown as exclusion—exclusion not from the village, but from the public sphere of urban life. Any realm dominated by upper castes, who though well-meaning and secular, is exclusive and casteist. He asks: How many upper caste people eat, informally,

---

[5] For a detailed reading of "Identity Card" see K. Satyanarayana and Susie Tharu, *No Alphabet in Sight* (New Delhi: Penguin, 2011), 1–3.

[6] See Satyanarayana and Tharu, *Steel Nibs are Sprouting*, 565–69.

at the homes of dalit friends? Why do upper caste people invariably fall in love with those of their own caste? He takes pains to demonstrate that even those 'good' and 'very good' people who consider themselves secular and modern actually participate in excluding dalits from the mainstream of Indian life. It is this kind of 'untouchability' that ensures that even educated and well-groomed dalits do not find a place in modern sectors such as the IT industry or the media, Chandra Bhan Prasad suggests. Govindaiah's "Letter to Father" is a moving poem that questions the promises of wealth and happiness that come with the new, independent India. Dalits have put their faith in these promises, but the rewards elude them always.

The complex relationship of dalits and modernity is a running theme in dalit writing. In Devanoora Mahadeva's masterpiece, "Tar Comes", modernity in the form of official 'development'—here a tarred road leading to the village—means little to the dalits who walk everywhere. In this case it also turns out that the tar brings death. But there is another modernity in the story that should not be missed. This is the modernity which the young educated dalits embrace and make use of—much to the discomfiture of the upper caste contractor. This is the modernity of the press, of a government that formally at least is accessible to everyone, and not least, the empowering modernity of education.

Dalit Christianity
Many dalit thinkers acknowledge the importance of Christian missionaries in raising questions of the equality of all people. Early dalit struggles for emancipation often involved conversion to Christianity. Education, self-respect and the possibility of mobility are associated with conversion. S. Joseph's "My Sister's Bible" points us to the specific and unusual relationship this young women has with that holy book that has lost all its 'official' pages. The tensions and contradictions of a young dalit Christian woman's experience is most complexly explored in M.M. Vinodini's "Parable of the Lost Daughter", which echoes the famous parable of the prodigal son but tells the story of a dalit girl whose education leaves her embarrassed by her people and their culture. She tries to brahminize herself, but is made all too

quickly to understand the hazards of that path. Her homecoming is a dalit Christian homecoming.

All the same, contemporary writers also point out that discrimination and even segregation exists within the Church and its institutions. Until a short while ago, in many parts of the country dalit Christians were not allowed into upper caste churches. Even today they remain marginal in the Church administration and in Christian institutions such as schools and hospitals. In "The Children of the Forest Talk to Yesu," M.B. Manoj refers to a struggle for access to the church graveyard which was hitherto not available to non-upper caste people.

Dalit Autobiographies

Dalit writing has given new life to autobiography. This is a genre that is focussed on an individual. It deals with his or her experiences, personality and feelings. Autobiographies are generally written by people who consider their life as one of importance or of significant personal achievement. Dalit autobiographies, critics argue, are quite different. In these stories, the individual's life acquires significance because it speaks of and for a community. It represents a group experience and is more like a testimony to that experience. In the early decades of the twentieth century in Kerala, testimonies of slaves, organized around the newly available notion of the suffering body, acquired central position in rituals associated with the Pratyaksha Raksha Daiva Sabha (PRDS). The historian Sanal Mohan argues that the idea that suffering is unjust and therefore of public significance in a democratic state, is connected with modern ideas of equality, freedom, and the good life.[7] Before this it was considered natural, and even just, that some people would suffer and live in pain and deprivation. That was their fate. With the coming of Western thinking and modern ideas, all this changed. For the first time, Mohan points out, the personal memory of untouchable slaves, and the feelings of sadness and outrage associated with those memories, were recognized as a source of truth and knowledge. Fifty years later, during the 1970s and after—broadly the

---

[7] For an elaboration of this, see Sanal Mohan, "Narrativising the History of Slave Suffering," in Satyanarayana and Tharu (ed.), *No Alphabet in Sight*, 535–55.

period that this collection deals with—autobiography, memoir and autobiographical fiction reappear as important forms of dalit writing. Dalit autobiographies are also personal stories, but these stories acquire special significance because they are not, at root, about the individual. On the contrary, they are important social and historical documents. The political philosopher Gopal Guru writes that they have the ability to turn terrible experiences into 'subversive chemicals'. Although some thinkers are critical of the new autobiographies which they dismiss as 'narratives of suffering', Guru considers dalit autobiographies as important because they illuminate the social world, provide new material for dalit politics and raise new questions for aesthetics.[8]

One of the best known and most widely translated autobiographies of recent times is Bama's *Karukku* (1992), which is an account of a dalit Christian girl from a Tamil Nadu village who grows up and joins a convent. Unwilling to put up with the discrimination she faces there, she leaves. This is an account of one person's life, but much of its significance lies in the fact that in many ways this life was shared by dalits making their way through the educational system and finding employment. Even when they receive family and government support, they face hostility and discrimination in many modes from their teachers, the administration and their fellow students. Baby Kamble's *Jina Amucha* (1986; trans. 2008 as *The Prisons We Broke*) is a document of a dalit woman's life in rural Maharashtra and the transformation effected by her encounter with Ambedkar and his thinking. Kumud Pawde actually says that her book (*Antasphot* [Outburst] 1981) should not be thought of as an autobiography. She creates the concept 'critical life narrative' to describe it. All dalit life stories are such narratives, she argues. When Pawde describes her struggle to become a Sanskrit scholar we realize that it is not enough for her to master the subject, she must make her way past prejudices that work like bundles of barbed wire placed across her path at different points. At every step, through exaggerated praise or subtle and obvious exclusion, she

[8] See Gopal Guru, "Review of *Joothan: A Dalit's Life* by Omprakash Valmiki" *Seminar*, October 2003, 70–71, and Ravikumar, *Venomous Touch: Notes on Caste, Culture and Politics* (Calcutta: Samya, 2009), 139–44.

is reminded that she is a dalit. Her autobiography also shows how difficult it is for dalits to actually get a job, despite reservations provided by the government. Some excuse is always found to avoid making the appointment. The fact that caste is pervasive does not mean that there are no positive experiences at all. Kumud Pawde mentions teachers and friends who helped her make her way through an otherwise hostile world.

The extract from Vasant Moon's autobiography, *Growing Up Untouchable in India*, first published in 1995, gives us a feel for the strength and skills of dalits, their pride in their abilities, the exuberant, yet civil way in which they traditionally conduct themselves. It also describes an incident which records the historical tension in the nationalist movement that is not often discussed in textbooks. This is the tension, discussed earlier, between those inspired by Ambedkar, who worked for the annihilation of caste, and Gandhians who believed that the caste order should remain although untouchability as a practice was wrong. In sum, then, it is important to read dalit autobiographies not as individual literary texts but as life stories written in the context of a movement to bring about change.

In addition to those mentioned above, historically important autobiographies, now available in English translation, are: Bama, *Karukku* (2001); Vasant Moon, *Growing Up Untouchable in India* (2001); Sharan Kumar Limbale, *Akkarmashi* (2003); Omprakash Valmiki, *Joothan* (2003); Narendra Jadhav, *The Outcaste* (2003); Aravind Malagatti, *Government Brahmana*, 2007; K.A. Gunasekaran, *Scar* (2009); Namdeo Nimgade, *In the Tiger's Shadow* (2010); Y.B. Satyanarayana, *My Father Balaiah*, (2011); and Siddalingaiah, *A Word With You, World* (2013). Sharmila Rege introduces us to autobiographical narratives by eight dalit women in *Writing Caste, Writing Gender: Narrating Dalit Women's Testimonios* (2006).

We need also to note that the term dalit writing as it is used today refers to literary as well as other writing done by dalits. Dalits bring points of view, interests, insights and directions that grow out of their experience and their aspirations. Over the past few decades this has transformed the understanding of untouchability, caste and the nature of Indian society and politics. Generally, though not always, dalit writing is also writing about dalits. In other words, dalit writers do not write only about dalits. They also write about many other things, and indeed about Indian life as a whole. It is the point of view and the understanding that they bring to the writing that makes it *dalit*. B. Krishnappa's essay in this collection explores these issues with originality and passion.

In conclusion: although it is possible to identify a few dalit writers from earlier times, the real originality and force of dalit writing, which today comprises a substantial and growing body of work, can be traced to the decades following the late 1960s. Those are the years when the Dalit Panthers re-visits and embraces the ideas of Babasaheb Ambedkar, and elaborates his disagreements with the essentially Gandhian mode of Indian nationalism, to begin a new social movement. In the following decades, dalit writing becomes an all-India phenomenon. This writing reformulates the caste question and reassesses the significance of colonialism and of missionary activity. It resists the reduction of caste to class or to non-brahminism and vividly describes and analyzes the contemporary workings of caste power.

REFERENCES

Dangle, Arjun, ed. *Poisoned Bread: Translations from Modern Marathi Dalit Literature*. Hyderabad: Orient Longman, 1992.

Guru, Gopal. "Review of *Joothan: A Dalit's Life* by Omprakash Valmiki." *Seminar*, October 2003, 70–71.

Mohan, Sanal. "Narrativising the History of Slave Suffering." In *No Alphabet in Sight*, edited by K. Satyanarayana and Susie Tharu, 535–55. New Delhi: Penguin, 2011.

Ravikumar. *Venomous Touch: Notes on Caste, Culture and Politics*. Calcutta: Samya, 2009.

Rege, Sharmila. "Introduction." In *Writing Caste, Writing Gender: Narrating Dalit Women's Testimonios*, 1–9. New Delhi: Zubaan, 2006.

Satyanarayana, K. and Susie Tharu, ed. *No Alphabet in Sight: New Dalit Writing from South India, Dossier 1: Tamil and Malayalam*. New Delhi: Penguin, 2011.

———, ed. *From those Stubs, Steel Nibs are Sprouting: New Dalit Writing from South India, Dossier 2: Kannada and Telugu*. New Delhi: HarperCollins, 2013.

B.R. AMBEDKAR

In March 1927, Dr Bhimrao Ramji Ambedkar (1891–1956)—scholar, political philosopher and India's foremost civil rights activist—led an agitation by dalits to draw water from the Chavadar lake in Mahad, Maharashtra. The water of this lake was hitherto reserved for caste Hindus. This historic event brought to the fore the fact that untouchables are not considered 'human' in India. In the second part of the Mahad satyagraha, on 25 December 1927, Ambedkar and his followers burnt a copy of the Manusmriti, *the second century* BCE *Hindu law code, as a mark of protest against Hinduism and untouchability. The following are excerpts from the speech he made on this occasion.*

WE TOO ARE HUMAN

Gentlemen, you have gathered here today in response to the invitation of the Satyagraha Committee. As chairman of that committee, I gratefully welcome you all.

Many of you will remember that on the 19th of last March all of us came to the Chavadar lake here. The caste Hindus of Mahad had laid no prohibition on us; but they showed they had objections to our going there by the attack they made. The fight brought results that one might have expected. The aggressive caste Hindus were sentenced to four months' rigorous imprisonment, and are now in jail. If we had not been hindered on the 19th of March, it would have been proved that the caste Hindus acknowledge our right to draw water from the lake, and we should have had no need to begin our present undertaking.

Unfortunately we were thus hindered, and we have been obliged to call this meeting today. This lake at Mahad is public property. The caste Hindus of Mahad are so reasonable that they not only draw water from the lake themselves but freely permit people of any religion to draw water from it, and accordingly people of other religions such as the Islamic do make use of this permission. Nor do the caste Hindus prevent members of species considered lower than the human, such as birds and beasts, from drinking at the lake. Moreover, they freely permit beasts kept by untouchables to drink at the lake. Caste Hindus are the very founts of compassion. They practise no hinsa and harass no one. They are not of the class of miserly and selfish folk who would grudge even a crow some grains of the food they are eating. The proliferation of sanyasis and mendicants is a living testimony to their charitable temperament. They regard altruism as religious merit and injury to another as a sin.

Even further, they have imbibed the principle that injury done by another must not be repaid but patiently endured, and so, they not only treat the harmless cow with kindness, but spare harmful creatures such as snakes. That one atman or spiritual self dwells in all creatures has become a settled principle of their conduct. Such are the caste Hindus who forbid some human beings of their own religion to draw water from the same Chavadar lake! One cannot help asking the question, why do they forbid us alone?

It is essential that all should understand thoroughly the answer to this question. Unless you do, I feel, you will not grasp completely the importance of today's meeting. The Hindus are divided, according to sacred tradition, into four castes; but according to custom, into five: brahmins, kshatriyas, vaishyas, shudras and atishudras. The caste system is the first of the governing rules of the Hindu religion. The second is that the castes are of unequal rank. They are ordered in a descending series of each meaner than the one before.

Not only are their ranks permanently fixed by the rule, but each is assigned boundaries it must not transgress, so that each one may at once be recognized as belonging to its particular rank. There is a general belief that the prohibitions in the Hindu religion against intermarriage, inter-dining, inter-drinking and social intercourse are bounds set to degrees of association with one another. But this is an incomplete idea. These prohibitions are indeed limits to degrees of association; but they have been set to show people of unequal rank what the rank of each is. That is, these bounds are symbols of inequality.

Just as the crown on a man's head shows he is a king, and the bow in his hand shows him to be a kshatriya, the class to which none of the prohibitions applies is considered the highest of all and the one to which they all apply is reckoned the lowest in rank. The strenuous efforts made to maintain the prohibitions are for the reason that, if they are relaxed, the inequality settled by religion will break down and equality will take its place.

The caste Hindus of Mahad prevent the untouchables from drinking the water of the Chavadar lake not because they suppose that the touch of the untouchables will pollute the water or that it will evaporate and vanish. Their reason for preventing the untouchables from drinking it is that they do not wish to acknowledge by such permission that castes declared inferior by sacred tradition are in fact their equals.

Gentlemen! You will understand from this the significance of the struggle we have begun. Do not let yourselves suppose that the Satyagraha Committee has invited you to Mahad merely to drink the water of the Chavadar lake of Mahad.

It is not as if drinking the water of the Chavadar lake will make us immortal. We have survived well enough all these days without drinking it. We are not going to the Chavadar lake merely to drink its water. We are going to the lake to assert that we too are human beings like others. It must be clear that this meeting has been called to set up the norm of equality. [...]

Some of you may feel that since we are untouchables, it is enough if we are set free from the prohibitions of inter-drinking and social intercourse. That we need not concern ourselves with the caste system; how does it matter if it remains? In my opinion this is a total error. If we leave the caste system alone and adopt only the removal of untouchability as our policy, people will say that we have chosen a low aim. To raise men, aspiration is needed as much as outward efforts. Indeed it is to be doubted whether efforts are possible without aspiration. Hence, if a great effort is to be made, a great aspiration must be nursed. In adopting an aspiration one need not be abashed or deterred by doubts about one's power to satisfy it. One should be ashamed only of mean aspirations; not of failure that may result because one's aspiration is high. If untouchability alone is removed, we may change from atishudras to shudras; but can we say that this radically removes untouchability? If such puny reforms as the removal of restrictions on social intercourse, etc., were enough for the eradication of untouchability, I would not have suggested that the caste system itself must go.

Gentlemen! You all know that if a snake is to be killed it is not enough to strike at its tail—its head must be crushed. If any harm is to be removed, one must seek out its root and strike at it. An attack must be based on the knowledge of the enemy's vital weakness. Duryodhana was killed because Bheema struck at his thigh with his mace. If the mace had hit Duryodhana's head he would not have died; for his thigh was his vulnerable spot. One finds many instances of a physician's efforts to remove a malady proving fruitless because he has not perceived fully what will get rid of the disease; similar instances of failure to root out a social disease because it is not fully diagnosed are rarely recorded in history; and so one does not often become aware of them. But let me acquaint you with one such instance that I have come across in my reading. In the ancient European nation of Rome, the patricians were considered upper class, and the plebeians, lower class. All power was in the hands of the patricians, and they used it to ill-treat the plebeians. To free themselves from this harassment, the plebeians, on the strength of their unity, insisted that laws should be written down for the facilitation of justice and for the information of all. Their patrician opponents agreed to this; and a charter of twelve laws was written down. But this did not rid the oppressed plebeians of their woes. For the officers who enforced the laws were all of the patrician class; moreover the chief officer, called the tribune, was also a patrician. Hence, though the laws were uniform, there was partiality in their enforcement. The plebeians then demanded that instead of the administration being in the hands of one tribune there should be two tribunes, of whom one should be elected by the plebeians and the other by the patricians. The patricians yielded to this too, and the plebeians rejoiced, supposing they would now be free of their miseries. But their rejoicing was short-lived. The Roman people had a tradition that nothing was to be done without the favourable verdict of the oracle at Delphi. Accordingly, even the election of a duly elected tribune—if the oracle did not approve of him—had to be treated as annulled, and another had to be elected, of whom the oracle approved. The priest who put the question to the oracle was required, by sacred religious custom, to be one born of parents married in the mode the Romans called 'conferatio'; and this mode of marriage prevailed only among the patricians; so that the priest of Delphi was always a patrician.

The wily priest always saw to it that if the plebeians elected a man really devoted to their cause, the oracle went against him. Only if the man elected by the plebeians to the position of tribune was amenable to the patricians, would the oracle favour him and give him the opportunity of actually assuming office. What did the plebeians gain by their right to elect a tribune? The answer must be, nothing in reality. Their efforts proved meaningless because they did not trace the malady to its source. If they had, they would, at the same time that they demanded a tribune of their election, have also settled the question of who should be the priest at Delphi. The disease could not be eradicated by demanding a tribune; it needed control of the priestly office, which the plebeians failed to perceive. We too, while we seek a way to remove untouchability, must inquire closely into what will eradicate the disease; otherwise we too may miss our aim. Do not be foolish enough to believe that removal of the restrictions on social intercourse or inter-drinking will remove untouchability.

Remember that if the prohibitions on social intercourse and inter-drinking go, the roots of untouchability are not removed. Release from these two restrictions will, at the most, remove untouchability as it appears outside the home; but it will leave untouchability in the home untouched. If we want to remove untouchability in the home as well as outside, we must break down the prohibition against intermarriage. Nothing else will serve. From another point of view, we see that breaking down the bar against intermarriage is the way to establish real equality. Anyone must confess that when the root division is dissolved, incidental points of separateness will disappear by themselves. The interdictions on inter-dining, inter-drinking and social intercourse have all sprung from the one interdiction against intermarriage. Remove the last and no special efforts are needed to remove the rest. They will disappear of their own accord. In my view the removal of untouchability consists in breaking down the ban on intermarriage and doing so will establish real equality. If we wish to root out untouchability, we must recognize that the root of untouchability is in the ban on intermarriage. Even if our attack today is on the ban against inter-drinking, we must press it home against the ban on intermarriage; otherwise untouchability cannot be removed by the roots. Who can accomplish this task? It is no secret that the brahmin class cannot do it.

While the caste system lasts, the brahmin caste has its supremacy. No one, of his own will, surrenders power that is in his hands. The brahmins have exercised their sovereignty over all other castes for centuries. It is not likely that they will be willing to give it up and treat the rest as equals. The brahmins do not have the patriotism of the samurais of Japan. It is useless to hope that they will sacrifice their privileges as the samurai class did, for the sake of national unity based on a new equality. Nor does it appear likely that the task will be carried out by other caste Hindus. These others, such as the class comprising the marathas and other similar castes, are a class between the privileged and those without any rights.

A privileged class, at the cost of a little self-sacrifice, can show some generosity. A class without any privileges has ideals and aspirations; for, at least as a matter of self-interest, it wishes to bring about a social reform. As a result it develops an attachment to principles rather than to self-interest. The class of caste Hindus other than brahmins lies in between: it cannot practise the generosity possible to the class above and it does not develop the attachment to principles that develops in the class below. This is why this class is seen to be concerned not so much about attaining equality with the brahmins as about maintaining its status above the untouchables.

For the purposes of the social reform required, the class of caste

Hindus other than brahmins is feeble. If we are to await its help, we should fall into the difficulties that the farmer faced, who depended on his neighbour's help for his harvesting, as in the story of the mother lark and her chicks found in many textbooks.

The task of removing untouchability and establishing equality that we have undertaken, we must carry out ourselves. Others will not do it. Our life will gain its true meaning if we consider that we are born to carry out this task and set to work in earnest. Let us receive this merit that is awaiting us.

This is a struggle in order to raise ourselves; hence we are bound to undertake it, so as to remove the obstacles to our progress. We all know how at every turn, untouchability muddies and soils our whole existence. We know that at one time our people were recruited in large numbers into the troops. It was a kind of occupation socially assigned to us, and few of us needed to be anxious about earning our bread. Other classes of our level have found their way into the troops, the police, the courts and the offices, to earn their bread. But in the same areas of employment you will no longer find the untouchables.

It is not that the law debars us from these jobs. Everything is permissible as far as the law is concerned. But the government finds itself powerless because other Hindus consider us untouchables and look down upon us, and it acquiesces in our being kept out of government jobs. Nor can we take up any decent trade. It is true, partly, that we lack money to start business, but the real difficulty is that people regard us as untouchables and no one will accept goods from our hands.

To sum up, untouchability is not a simple matter; it is the mother of all our poverty and lowliness and it has brought us to the abject state we are in today. If we want to raise ourselves out of it, we must undertake this task. We cannot be saved in any other way. It is a task not for our benefit alone; it is also for the benefit of the nation.

Hindu society must sink unless the untouchability that has become a part of the four-castes system is eradicated. Among the resources that any society needs in the struggle for life, a great resource is the moral order of that society. And everyone must admit that a society in which the existing moral order upholds things that disrupt the society and condemns those that would unite the members of the society, must find itself defeated in any struggle for life with other societies. A society that has the opposite moral order, one in which things that unite are considered laudable and things that divide are condemned, is sure to succeed in any such struggle.

This principle must be applied to Hindu society. Is it any wonder that it meets defeat at every turn when it upholds a social order that fragments its members, though it is plain to anyone who sees it that the four-castes system is such a divisive force and that a single caste for all, would unite society? If we wish to escape these disastrous conditions, we must break down the framework of the four-castes system and replace it by a single caste system.

Even this will not be enough. The inequality inherent in the four-castes system must be rooted out. Many people mock at the principles of equality. Naturally, no man is another's equal. One has an impressive physique; another is slow-wined. The mockers think that, in view of these inequalities that men are born with, the egalitarians are absurd in telling us to regard them as equals. One is forced to say that these mockers have not understood fully the principle of equality.

If the principle of equality means that privilege should depend, not on birth, wealth, or anything else, but solely on the merits of each man, then how can it be demanded that a man without merit, and who is dirty and vicious, should be treated on a level with a man who has merit and is clean and virtuous? Such is a counter-question sometimes posed. It is essential to define equality as giving equal privileges to men of equal merit.

But before people have had an opportunity to develop their inherent qualities and to merit privileges, it is just to treat them all equally. In sociology, the social order is itself the most important factor in the full development of qualities that any person may possess at birth. If slaves are constantly treated unequally, they will develop no qualities other than those appropriate to slaves, and they will never become fit for any higher status. If the clean man always repulses the unclean man and refuses to have anything to do with him, the unclean man will never develop the aspiration to become clean. If the criminal or immoral castes are given no refuge by the virtuous castes, the criminal castes will never learn virtue.

The examples given above show that, although an equal treatment may not create good qualities in one who does not have them at all, even such qualities where they exist need equal treatment for their development; also, developed good qualities are wasted and frustrated without equal treatment.

On the one hand, the inequality in Hindu society stunts the progress of individuals and in consequence stunts society. On the other hand, the same inequality prevents society from bringing into use powers stored in individuals. In both ways, this inequality is weakening Hindu society, which is in disarray because of the four-castes system.

Hence, if Hindu society is to be strengthened, we must uproot the four-castes system and untouchability, and set the society on the foundations of the two principles of one caste only and of equality. The way to abolish untouchability is not any other than the way to invigorate Hindu society. Therefore I say that our work is beyond doubt as much for the benefit of the nation as it is in our own interest.

Our work has been begun to bring about a real social revolution. Let no one deceive himself by supposing that it is a diversion to quieten minds entranced with sweet words. The work is sustained by strong feeling, which is the power that drives the movement. No one can now arrest it. I pray to god that the social revolution that begins here today may fulfil itself by peaceful means.

None can doubt that the responsibility of letting the revolution take place peacefully rests more heavily on our opponents than on us. Whether this social revolution will work peacefully or violently will depend wholly on the conduct of the caste Hindus. People who blame the French National Assembly of 1789 for atrocities forget one thing. That is, if the rulers of France had not been treacherous to the Assembly, if the upper classes had not resisted it, had not committed the crime of trying to suppress it with foreign help, it would have had no need to use violence in the work of the revolution and the whole social transformation would have been accomplished peacefully.

We say to our opponents too: please do not oppose us. Put away the orthodox scriptures. Follow justice. And we assure you that we shall carry out our programme peacefully.

Transcribed by Changdeo Khairmode
Translated from Marathi by Rameshchandra Sirkar

SIDDALINGAIAH

Siddalingaiah (1954–), a leading Kannada poet and public intellectual, is one of the founders of the Dalit Sangharsha Samiti and played a significant role in the dalit movement in Karnataka in the 1970s and 1980s. Siddalingaiah participated in the boosa agitation of the mid-70s. Lyrics from his first collection, Holemaadigara Haadu *(Songs of the Holeya and Madiga, 1975), often sung at public meetings and demonstrations by the famous Janardhan (Jenni), were heralded as path-breaking. He has since published several other collections of poetry and an autobiography,* Ooru Keri, *in two parts (rendered in English as* A Word With You, World: The Autobiography of a Poet, *2013). He has been the head of Department of Kannada at Bangalore University and a member of the Legislative Council. He is currently chairman, Kannada Book Authority.*

THOUSANDS OF RIVERS

Yesterday
they came like a mountain
did my people.

Dark faces, silvery beards, smouldering eyes
tearing day and night apart, kicking sleep goodbye.
Blankets shivered at their waking;
the earth shook under their feet.

Marching like ants, roaring like lions
Down with inequality!
Forever down with
the arrogance of the rich!

Like countless snakes they crawled in
and filled the town;
descended to the lower depths
soared high in the sky.

In the streets and the lanes
under trees and by the fences
in the landlord's house, on the master's throne
everywhere they flowed like water
did my people.
When they opened their mouths
the others fell silent.
Listening to their voices
the other throats dried up.

With their waving arms they stirred up
a storm of revolution,
did my people.
They caught by the neck those
who had beaten them with sticks.

Police lathis, agents' knives,
barrels of guns,
vedas shastras puranas
all floated like dry leaves.

Thousands of rivers to
the sea of struggle.

THE DALITS ARE COMING

The dalits are coming, step aside—
hand over the reins, let them rule.

Minds burning with countless dreams,
slogans like thunder and lightning,
in the language of earthquakes,
here comes the dalit procession,
writing [history] with their feet.

Into the dump go gods and gurus,
down the drain go the lawmakers.

On a path they struck for themselves
March the dalits in procession,
burning torches in their hands,
sparks of revolution in their eyes
exploding like balls of fire.

For the thorn bushes of caste and religion,
they were as thorns in the side.
They became the sky that looked down at
the seven seas that swallowed them.

Since Rama's time and Krishna's time
unto the time of the Gandhis,
They had bowed low with folded hands.
Now they have risen in struggle.

It grows, it breaks out of its shell
the endless dalit procession.
Bullet for bullet, blood for blood,
shoulder to shoulder, lives bound together.

Under the flag of dalit India
stood the farmers and workers.
Flowers bloom in every forest,
thousands of birds take flight,
the eastern sky turned red,
morning broke for the poor.

The dalits are coming, step aside!
The dalits have come, give it up!

Translated from Kannada by M. Madhava Prasad

T.H.P. CHENTHARASSERY

T.H.P Chentharassery (1928–) was born into a family of considerable social standing: his grandmother and father defied casteism to secure rights for the community. His father, Thiruvan, was a local organiser of the Sadhu-jana Paripalana Sangham formed under the leadership of Ayyankali in 1907. Chentharassery, who had a B.Com.—a very high qualification at that time—received work only as a clerk. He taught himself history, and wrote over thirty books, some of which are yet to be published. His Ayyankali (1979) is the first study on Ayyankali, the forgotten dalit revolutionary of Kerala. Dr Ambedkar: Thatva Chinthayun Pravarthanangulam *(Dr Ambedkar: Philosophy and Practice, 1990)* and The History of Indigenous Indians *(1998) are among his best known works.*

AYYANKALI AND THE SADHUJANA PARIPALANA SANGHAM THE STORY OF A FREEDOM MOVEMENT

A hysterical frenzy infects new converts who tend to become zealots of their new faith. The puthuchristianikal (new[ly converted] Christians) of south Kerala were not an exception. They looked down upon their kinsfolk who had joined the Hindu mutt sangham set up by Swami Sadananda, a reformed nair sanyasi from north Kerala. The converts outdid the orthodox Christians in defending their new faith and proclaiming Jesus. For them, those who followed other religions were godless pagans. These white-clad, Bible-flaunting puthuchristianikal made it a point to taunt and mock their unconverted kinsfolk. The devotees of the mutt sangham found themselves between the devil and the deep sea. On the one hand, they were losing their ties and sense of community with their Christian kinsfolk. On the other, the mutt sangham with its focus on transcendent spirituality let them down on the socio-economic plane. Ayyankali and his men finally resolved to secede from the ineffectual mutt sangham.

The new converts to Christianity also found their great expectations blocked by the discriminations of upper castes within the Christian fold. The anti-untouchability movement led by educated converts like V.J. Thomas Vadhyar and Harris Vadhyar began to catch on. The movement gradually broadened its base encompassing both Christian and non-Christian untouchables, finally leading to the formation of Sadhujana Paripalana Sangham or SJPS in 1907 with the bold and fearless Ayyankali as its undisputed leader.

Ayyankali was fortunately free from sub-caste prejudices. His goal was the emancipation of all untouchables. That was why he was able to enlist the support of all untouchable sub-castes: pulaya, paraya and kurava. Poykayil Yohannan (Shri Kumara Gurudevan), the founder of Prathyaksha Raksha Daiva Sabha or PRDS (1910) and a contemporary of Ayyankali, was another great leader who united people across sub-caste divisions. Unfortunately, Ayyankali's movement in later years lost its edge against sub-caste divisiveness and shrank into a single-caste organization.

It is obvious that Ayyankali sought and received assistance from a number of philanthropists and reformers well-versed in social transactions. Educated members of SJPS like Thomas Vadhyar took care of the propaganda, drafting of memorials, correspondence and clerical matters. A constitution containing the aims and objectives as well as the rules and regulations of the organization was adopted. It emphasized the virtues of cleanliness and discipline on the part of the members, and enshrined goals such as the freedom of movement, the right to education and proper clothing and so on. The resemblance that the name of the organization bears to Sree Narayana Dharma Paripalanayogam or SNDP (1903) suggests the influence of individuals and organizations with a reformist agenda.

The Sangham demanded a six-day week for workers and resolved to observe Sunday as a holiday. The community met on Sundays to discuss and reflect on their problems. Annual subscriptions were collected from members to the tune of half a chakram for men and a quarter for women. Money thus collected for three years was used to meet the expense of getting the Sangham registered with the government.

The Sangham agenda accorded top priority to the question of education. Thomas Vadhyar had already taken initiatives in this regard by submitting a number of memorials to the authorities concerned. A government order favouring the entry of untouchable children to schools was issued in 1907 thanks to the intervention of P. Rajagopalachari, the then diwan of Travancore. But casteism rather than good sense prevailed and the authorities deferred the implementation of the order. Somehow or the other, the Sangham got scent of this and started demanding admission to schools. Ayyankali went from school to school knocking at their gates in vain. This was a demand the caste Hindus could hardly be expected to put up with. They resisted with all their might. The upper-caste notions of purity and status stood in the way. Their children could not sit in the same classroom as the untouchables. Abomination! Pollution! Insubordination! Unable to brook this affront to their vanity, the caste Hindus defied the government order.

Ayyankali was enraged by this blatant act of caste oppression. He stood his ground. Neither opposition nor fate would hold him down. He braced himself to confront the upper castes. Tit for tat, he thought. "If you won't admit our children to schools, your lands will lie fallow and grow weeds," declared Ayyankali, threatening strike on their farms. His gritty words had the force of a vow that snapped all the so-called 'idyllic relations' between the janmi [landlord] and his adiyan [bondsman].

The sky of south Kerala grew murky. Dark clouds of unrest gathered. The Sangham under the leadership of Ayyankali demanded better wages and an immediate end to tyranny vis-à-vis the untouchables. They called upon the government to relieve the people from police brutalities perpetrated on grounds of framed charges. They reiterated their cries for freedom of movement and right to education. We can call these demands a yearning for human dignity. Untouchables were yet to be accorded the status of human beings.

A spate of confrontations followed. The stand-off between the janmis and the untouchables went on indefinitely. The unabated hostility affected the livelihood of the untouchables. Still they refused to give in. One day, Ayyankali addressed his people thus: "The country can progress only through us who are workers on lands. If we strike work, our masters will starve. We are used to starvation and we don't care. Let us strike work from tomorrow."

The strike was on. It spread across the lands of the upper castes through the neighbouring villages of Kandala, Kaniyapuram, Pallichal, up to Vizhinjam. The workers stood solid behind Ayyankali despite threats of violence, murder and arson. A militia called Ayyankalippada was constituted by men trained in martial arts, for defending the people. The landowners also took measures to counter the rebellion. They swore to suppress the revolt at any cost. A vigilante gang was formed under the captaincy of a prominent nair janmi called Puthalathu Krishna Pillai. The landowners held out carrots and brandished sticks to encourage dissension and backsliding among workers. But Ayyankalippada defeated those stratagems by dissuading the workers from turning blacklegs.

The prolongation of the strike had its impact on both sides. The janmis were unable to cultivate their lands. The workers were unable to find their livelihood. But Ayyankali was adamant. Then a clever idea occurred to him. He thought of finding alternative jobs for the striking workers. For this, he made a pact with the fisherfolk of Vizhinjam who agreed to take some of the strikers along with them on their fishing expeditions. This was a tactical victory for the workers. The janmis, in their sense of defeat, ran amok. The workers retaliated. And the government had to intervene to stop the violence.

Diwan P. Rajagopalachari took the initiative to bring about a negotiated settlement. He appointed Kandala Nagam Pillai, a first class magistrate as the mediator. The janmis conceded the demand for increase in wages and agreed to be lenient about school entry and freedom of movement. The year-long agrarian struggle ended in 1908. Seven years later, Ayyankali recalled this event as he addressed a reconciliation meeting in Kollam after the Perinadu riots had broken out on the issue of the right of untouchable women to decent dress (*Mithavadi*, January 1916).

The first labour strike in the history of Kerala brought about an attitudinal change among the untouchables, especially the youth. They became less deferential towards their feudal lords. The upper castes swallowed their pride and plotted the destruction of Ayyankali. A reward of Rs 2,000 was offered for catching him alive and Rs 1,000 for fetching him dead. But Ayyankali carried on undaunted, unmindful of the feudal conspiracy. Mr Mitchel, the director of education, was an Englishman interested in the uplift of the untouchables. He reminded the diwan about the government order of 1907 that had been swept under the carpet. As a result, a new order was issued in 1910, granting school entry to untouchables. That the reaction of the upper-caste public was hostile is quite obvious from the way Ramakrishna Pillai, editor of *Swadeshabhimani*, responded to the issue of school entry.

For him, it was a measure without rhyme or reason. Drawing a distinction between those who cultivate their intellect and those who cultivate the land, he compared it to yoking the horse and the buffalo to the same plough (*Swadeshabhimani*, 2 March 1910). Ramakrishna Pillai was not merely an editor, but a rebel, a progressive, and a firebrand critic of the establishment. He is also credited with the first biography of Karl Marx in Malayalam.

Emboldened by the government order of 1910, people approached local schools to enrol their children. The schools continued their posture of defiance. When Ayyankali reached the school at Ooruttampalam holding a little girl called Panchami by the hand, a bevy of criminals and goondas had been positioned to block their way. "If an untouchable is admitted, we will torch the school," shrieked Kochappi Pillai, leader of the ruffians. The upper castes took law into their hands and set the school on fire.

Riots broke out. Rape and arson, lootings and street fights went on for seven days. Though it subsided in Ooruttampalam, its ripples spread far and wide. "One of the disturbances that occurred during the reign of Shri Moolam Thirunal is the 'pulaya lahala'. These riots spread in and around the Neyyattinkara taluk. It was the most grievous of all riots at that time," wrote Velupillai in the *Travancore State Manual* (Vol. II).

Historians with a certain bias considered the first war of Indian independence to be the Sepoy Mutiny [in Malayalam, *Sipayi Lahala*]. No wonder then that upper-caste historians did not have a better word than 'lahala' to describe the first freedom struggle of the untouchables.

Ayyankali's call for a labour strike occurred long before the arrival of Marxism and trade unionism. The Russian Revolution was still in its incipient stage. The strike was a weapon of struggle unheard of in this part of the world at that time. This epic strike of the most oppressed among the oppressed that took place in an obscure corner of south Kerala deserves a niche in the wall of world history.

Translated from Malayalam by T.M. Yesudasan

M.B. MANOJ

M.B. Manoj (1972–) has emerged as an important Malayalam poet and thinker. He played a leading role in SFI and later moved away to work extensively with the Maoist CPI(ML). After 1991, with the Maoist movements going into decline, he moved towards Ambedkarite- Buddhist thought. Manoj actively worked in the Dalit Vidhyarthi Ekopana Samiti and also joined the Kurichi reading group associated with Dalit Women's Society. Among his published collections of poetry are: Oottandhathayude Ezhupathu Varshangal (Seventy Years of Deep Blindness, 2005) and Kaanunnillorak-sharavum (No Alphabet in Sight, 2007).

THE CHILDREN OF THE FOREST TALK TO YESU

We are not the ones who whipped you;
we even gave our land to hang your pictures
and adorn your statues
that lean forward from the Cross.

Why, Yesu, instead of talking straight,
did you ever lead us along
this tortuous path?

Tell us the truth:
aren't You really
our betrayer?

You might have lived for
your twelve disciples;
what is that to us?

Here, on this churchyard,
Your devotees screamed with the same tongue
that had offered you prayers:
'This man is a tribal.

Throw him to the police.'
Yesu,
for which side did you then pray?

Does he/she
have any way left to freely walk,
be clothed,
to fall asleep?

We kept moving away,
farther away, as they drove us,
to the very edges of the earth.
Yet you keep returning
as People's Man,
as newspapers,
as The Public and as old rag.

Today, watching the nakedness
of your fair body, yet unburied,
let us speak the unsullied words
of the confessors:

'We will not hand over this land
even if four hundred thousand dead
are laid to rest.
Praise be!'

ANONYMOUS

I remember how father used to scrub me
with a stone while washing me so that
I might become fair.
Now he burns in the heavy rain;
mother rots in the noonday sun.
Still my younger brother leaps up
gazing at the kite
the wind's teeth have torn to pieces.

When the floods came
I longed to make
a little paper-boat
to flee the drowning land.
Another time, when
fire devoured my house,
I only prayed
it should not burn down
the toy fawn,
that it may safely reach its mother.
And, since she had not come to hear
about my short neck and rough hands,
the honeycomb, the porcupine's quills
and the crow's twig may be returned
where they belonged.

Translated from Malayalam by K. Satchidanandan

VASANT MOON

Vasant Moon (1932–2002) was a civil servant and a dalit activist born in Nagpur, Maharashtra. His autobiography, Vasti *(1995) was the first dalit autobiography to be published in English (as* Growing Up Untouchable in India, *2001) from which the following excerpt is taken. A staunch Ambedkarite, he edited seventeen volumes of Dr Ambedkar's writings and speeches in English. These were published by the Education Department, Government of Maharashtra.*

GROWING UP UNTOUCHABLE IN INDIA

Many activities went on in the community, especially sports. Wrestling grounds and hututu [kabaddi] sprouted everywhere in Nagpur. The boys of the community were dexterous in both. In the beginning they took part in marches of the Maratha Lancers; later the Ahirrao Club sponsored them at the palace of the Bhosles. The Maratha Mandal and the Bhosle Club also sponsored competitions. However, the mahar vastis were not lagging behind. Tournaments were held at Bhankhed; matches were organized by Chitaman Kamble at Babhulkhed, and at Gita Grounds and Handicraft Grounds in Bardi. And at Katnathi, competitions were held every year on the memorial day of Haridas L.N.

When our Bhagyodaya Club reached the finals of the Maratha Lancers' competition in 1939, all the Nagpurites gathered to see the match. As the passion for hututu grew, youth of all ages had started taking part in the matches. Hututu matches were held in the Cokhamela hostel in the new colony beside the railway lines. The hostel had been established around 1925 by Nanasaheb Gavai, Kisan Fagoji Bansode, and other mahar activists with the help of Shahu Maharaj of Kolhapur. The Bardi group decided to send not simply one but two teams. And so the players were split up.

The players in the Bhagyodaya Club seemed each taller than

the other. Most were six to six and a half feet tall. When Fattu Gajbhiye of the A team came out, not a single man would escape without being beaten. Fattu Rangari was tall but thin and wiry, agile as a cheetah. Big Nathu Shende was potbellied. He was magnificently stout, and if he was caught he would take two to four with him. When Uncle Pralhad or Goma Sontakke guarded the corner, anyone who went inside had no hope of coming out. Along with Bodad Rangari, Yogi Mohil, Pundalik Rangari, and Hari Khobragade to make a military array, this was the A team.

But the B team was not inferior. Actually, once the A team was formed, a B team was not required. But they wanted to give all the players a chance, and so the B team was created. This team had wrestler Mahadev Gajbhiye, whose grasp was fabled; Atmaram Paithankar, who was very black and agile as a snake; Macchindra Mohite, whose stride could catch one at any time; the short brothers Pandurang and Bhanudas Varade, with strong grips; wrestler Tukaram Varade; Premchand Godbole, who shouted abuses and remained enthusiastic to the end; Sadashiv Sontakke; Maroti Bagade; Paiku Shende; the six-footer Govind Meshram; Changdev Meshram; and the dexterous Changdev Vasnik.

The competition began in the courtyard of the Cokhamela hostel, and the Sitabardi folk went to see the prowess of their boys. One game after another took place, but neither team of Bardi appeared ready to retreat. The semifinal rounds came, and both teams won in their class. The next Sunday would see the final match, and this match would be between the A and B teams of the Bhagyodaya Club. With enthusiasm mounting among the spectators, the players returned home.

Naturally, the A team was considered superior to B. However, the B team was determined to make an assault. Both began to practice morning and evening. They started hurling taunts at each other coming and going on the roads. Debates erupted, and wagers were made.

On Sunday there was no place to stand at the Cokhamela hostel grounds. Enthusiasm was at a boiling point. All of Bardi had gathered to see the match. But in those days spectators were disciplined. No match before this had seen such self-restraint. Even with competition there was no quarrelling, no fighting. The athletes split off one man after another in a disciplined way up to the end. And the whistle to end the match was blown. People stared in surprise. The A team had been defeated by the B team!

But the real victory was that of Bardi's Bhagyodaya Club, not that of any individual. Both teams took their shields of awards for the final and semifinal rounds and returned in procession to Bardi, tossing the flowers of their victory garlands as they went. The whole community that day was bathed in joy.

The photo of the shield won that day by Bardi's Maharpura is kept even today in many houses.

In 1941 the Cokhamela hostel management, with the collaboration of some harijan students, decided to call Mahatma Gandhi for the hostel annual gathering. Most of the students, who were strong Ambedkarites and activists of the Samata Sainik Dal, opposed this. However, no one was in the mood to listen. Sadanand Dongare lived in the hostel, but he felt he could not vanquish the idea of bringing Gandhi while staying there. One or two kilometers away from the hostel towards the railway lines, there stood a hostel for mahars named Gaddi Godam. He took a room there and laid out all his plans. The youth of north and central Nagpur came together.

By the day of Mahatma Gandhi's planned arrival, a huge pavilion had been erected in the central area of the hostel's open ground. A strong line of police was placed outside. Nanasaheb Gavai, Kisan Fagoji Bansode, and other mahar opponents of Ambedkar were members of the managing board. The president was Chaturbhajabhai Jasani of Gondiya. He was a loyal member of the Congress and a great leader of Madhya Pradesh. He brought Mahatma Gandhi from Delhi, but he took him off the train two stations early, and because of this the Ambedkarite community, which was spread throughout Nagpur, was led to believe that Gandhi had not come. However, Gandhiji had come to Nagpur in the company of Jasani.

On the east side of the Cokamela hostel lay a parallel railway line running north-south. This line goes via Itwara, Katol, and Kalm-eshwar to Delhi and east to Calcutta. Stone rocks had fallen on the railway line. Women and men, young and old gathered on this line, and shouted, "Long live Ambedkar!" On the north, south, and west of the hostel lay people's houses and narrow roads.

Mahatma Gandhi's car came to the hostel from behind. There the members of the reception committee were waiting to welcome him. While they were trying to shout "Long live Gandhi," a noise like one voice could be heard from the thousands of demonstrators outside: "Mahatma Gandhi go back!" And as this noise reached the neighbour-hoods around, people began to run towards the hostel.

The hostel was a four-sided block two hundred by two hundred feet in size. The pavilion had been set up in the open ground in the middle. Here, along with the students of the hostel, distinguished guests had been invited to sit. But there were many Ambedkarite dalits among the students. Until Gandhiji went onto the stage, everything was quiet inside. But once he rose to speak, some of the Ambedkarite students in the audience stood up and began to shout, "Gandhiji, we have many questions for you." Gandhiji was standing quietly. He said, "Yes, ask them." But the turmoil only increased. No one could hear the questions in that confusion. The hundreds of people standing outside on the railway lines began a massive stone-throwing into the hostel. The stones fell inside the pavilion also. There was no sign of halting this attack. Once the stones hit the canvas, it began to collapse. No one would give Gandhi a chance to make his speech. In this confusion, the organizers brought Gandhiji out of the pavilion to protect him. Just as he had come in by the back door, so he left.

With the shouting of "Long live Ambedkar! Bhim Raj is coming soon!" Mahatma Gandhi's car departed. People lifted up Sakharani Meshram, who was trying to quiet them down, and tried to throw him in a well. At that point Narayan Hari Kumbhare intervened to try to calm people down. The incident showed the ferocity of the anti-Gandhi sentiments of the people.

Translated from Marathi by Gail Omvedt

ANNA BHAU SATHE

Born into the mang community in Maharashtra, Anna Bhau Sathe (1920–69) was denied schooling on account of his caste. Notwithstanding his lack of formal education, he published a formidable body of literature, spanning four plays, thirty-two novels, thirteen collections of short stories, eleven ballads (povadé, in Marathi) and a travelogue. He harnessed the power of folk theatre to create social awareness through tamashas and povadé, defying, at one point, Home Minister Morarji Desai's ban on tamashas by renaming them loknatya. He inaugurated the first Dalit Literary Conference in 1958. Fondly remembered as 'Lok Shahir' (people's poet), Sathe was an avowed communist, dedicated to the destruction of both the caste and class structures of society.

GOLD FROM THE GRAVE

Bheema was excited by the news of the death and burial of a prominently wealthy man in the neighbouring village. He was elated and in his imagination he visited the man in the grave several times over. Sitting under a tamarind tree he watched Nabda, his darling daughter, playing by herself. His wife cooked the meal inside and Bheema waited for the sunset and the dark. He glanced eagerly at the sun, which was not going down fast enough for him.

Bheema was built like a giant. When going out he usually put on a yellowish dhoti, a red turban and a shirt of coarse cloth. He looked like a wrestler. With his big, bulky head, thick neck, bushy eyebrows and broad face sporting a luxuriant growth of moustache, he had frightened many a ruffian into docility. He feared nothing.

Bheema was from a village on the banks of the river Warna. His great strength was of no help in him in finding a job in his own village. He had strayed over to Bombay in search of work. He had searched for a job all over the city in vain and finally moved to this suburb on the fringe of the jungle. His dream of having a gold necklace made for his wife had come to nothing. He hated the city of Bombay, which offers you everything except work and shelter. Settling in the suburb he landed a job as a stone quarry worker.

The jungle had given him both gainful employment and a roof over his head. With his strength of a giant he attacked the rocks, and the hill receded. Granite rocks gaped wide open at the strokes of his hammer. His employer, the gnarly contractor, appreciated his work and Bheema was quite happy with his job.

Within six months the quarry closed down and Bheema found himself without work. It was a shock for him to learn that he was job-less when he reported for duty one morning. He was confused. The thought of starvation plunged him into the deepest pit of anxiety. He stood by the side of a stream in the jungle with his clothes under his arm. He washed himself and started walking towards home. Look-ing around he found that there were mounds of ashes, obviously the remains of funeral pyres, and charred bones scattered everywhere. The thought of death did not frighten him. He thought that the dead person must have been jobless, and death must have given him relief. He knew that starvation was staring him in the face. His darling Nabda would go on crying for food, his wife would be sullen, and he would have to watch all this helplessly.

Suddenly he noticed something sparkle on the top of the mound of ashes and he bent forward to have a closer look. It was a ring of gold weighing about twelve grams and he quickly picked it up. Squeezing the ring in his palm he felt the keen pleasure of a discovery. Finding gold in the ashes of a funeral pyre opened a way for Bheema to survive and keep the wolf at bay.

The next day found him wandering all over in search of crema-tion grounds and graveyards. Sifting the ashes he gleaned grains of gold. Seldom did he return home without an earring, a nose ring, an anklet or a necklace. He found that the intense heat of the funeral pyre melts the gold, which gets embedded in the bones. He shattered the charred bones into small pieces. Ruthlessly he reduced the skulls and wrist bones to powder to find a grain of the precious metal. In the evening he went to Kurla, a suburb of Bombay, sold the gold and returned with money in his pocket. On his way home he usually bought a packet of dates for his darling Nabda.

Bheema thus lived by sifting the ashes of dead bodies. He could not understand this paradox of life and death. The distinction between the two was lost on him. He knew that there was gold in the ashes of a rich person, and that the ashes of a poor man did not contain a grain of the metal. His simple logic led him to believe that only the rich should die to help the poor live in this world and that a poor man has no right to die. Day and night he searched cremation grounds and graveyards. Like a ghoul he lived on corpses and so his life was inextricably woven with corpses.

Strange happenings were being reported at that time. Corpses buried in tombs were found to be exhumed. The dead body of a young daughter-in-law of a moneylender was said to have been hauled to the river bank from the burial ground. This causes panic among the people. The police were alerted. It wasn't, however, easy to guard the corpses in the graveyard. An all-night vigil over the cemetery was impossible.

The sun set and now it was dark. Bheema ate the food served by his wife. Divining his intentions she asked him where he was set for. "Let's give up this business," she expostulated. "The whole thing is disgusting. This sifting of ashes, the corpses, the gold, everything is ghastly. People have started talking about us," she said.

"Shut up," Bheema shouted at her. Feeling hurt he said in a peevish tone, "I'll do what I like. Let people say what they will. Who'll feed us if I don't earn?"

"Please don't misunderstand me. This kind of wandering in the cemetery like a fiend is not a fitting occupation for you. I'm frightened to death. The whole thing gives me the creeps."

"Who's told you that ghosts only haunt graveyards?" retorted Bheema. "This city of Bombay itself is a colony of ghosts. The real spectres live in houses and the dead ones rot in the graves. Monsters breed in the city, not in the jungles." Bheema concluded.

This silenced her and Bheema prepared himself for the night's excursion. He growled at his wife that he had not got a job while he roamed all over Bombay, but the funeral ashes had brought him gold. "When I broke stone the whole day I received only a couple of rupees while a day's work on the funeral ashes fetches me a tenner." He left home in anger. It was quiet everywhere when Bheema started on his night round.

He had covered his head with a piece of cloth and draped himself with the cowl of a gunnybag. Having girdled his waist Bheema walked on with long strides, holding a pointed iron bar under his arm. All around him it was pitch dark but Bheema was not afraid. The only thought in his mind was that of buying a sari, a petticoat and a blouse and a packet of dates.

The atmosphere was charged with expectancy. The silence was oppressive. A pack of jackals scampered away after a piercing howl. A snake wound away from the path into the jungle. An owl screeched and the silence grew more frightening. Bheema approached the village and squatting down, peered all over. The village was very quiet. Someone coughed, a lamp winked and everything was still again. Bheema was satisfied. He entered the cemetery and looked for the most recent burial mound. He jumped from one to the other. Scattering the broken earthen pots and bamboo strips he lighted a safety match at each mound and made for the rich man's grave.

Clouds gathered in the sky. The darkness deepened and there was a crack of lightning. Bheema was scared at the prospect of rain, for it might not then be possible for him to find the newly dug grave.

Quickly he moved on and the effort made him perspire. On reaching the end he was frightened and stopped dead. He heard the gnashing of teeth. The sounds of growling and scratching of the earth were also audible. Bheema could not understand it. He lurched forward and all was quiet again. In a short while he heard somebody kicking and Bheema was struck with fear. It was for the first time in his life that he experienced dread, this fear of the supernatural.

But he soon collected himself. When he realized what was happening he felt ashamed. A pack of jackals was there for the dead body buried in the grave. They did not touch the stones laid on the ground.

They were trying to reach the corpse by burrowing through the sides. Having scented flesh they were ravenously attacking the grave in which the recently dead man was buried. Though united in their goal they were in furious competition with one another. Putting their noses to the ground they sniffed and vigorously assailed the grave, having been excited by the scent of flesh.

Bheema was furious. He jumped onto the top of the mound and stationed himself amidst the stones on the rich man's grave. Bheema picked up the large stones and hurled them at the jackals. This sudden attack frightened them and they moved away into hiding.

Bheema, encouraged, decided to get to the corpse before the jackals did.

When the jackals found him busy at work they attacked him. One charged at him, as if in a frenzy, and snapped at his gunnybag cover. Bheema was upset that his cover was torn. Spitting out the pieces of the gunnybag stuck in its fangs, the jackal charged at Bheema with greater vehemence. Now Bheema was ready for it. He finished the animal with one jab of the pointed crowbar. With the fallen animal lying dead by his side, Bheema began digging the grave. But the jackals in the pack attacked him from all sides and a dreadful battle ensued.

Bheema had unearthed half the tomb but had to pause awhile to defend himself against the jackals who were snapping at his flesh. He gave a blow to each one that attacked him. The jackals fell when he hit them but others hurled themselves upon him in greater fury and tore at his muscles.

Bheema, who bore the name of the second son of Kunti, was fighting the jackals for the possession of a carcass, his daily bread. A grim battle was fought in the vicinity of the village, a battle that would never be recorded in the annals of the country's mythology.

All over it was quiet. The city of Bombay was asleep and the village, at rest. The macabre war in the graveyard raged on. The man fought for the gold and the beasts for their food.

Bheema hit the animals with his pointed iron bar and felled them. Those that escaped his jabs tore at his flesh and those that were hit screamed aloud. Bheema howled in pain when he was bitten and swore at them.

After a very long time, the jackals stopped their attack for some moments of rest. Seeing this, Bheema began his work of digging open the grave. He loosened the earth and wiped the sweat off his face. He was utterly exhausted. No sooner did he get down into the tomb than the pack of jackals again charged at him. He struck them hard and the defeated pack scampered away. Bheema, the giant, had come out victorious because of his strength and endurance.

Bheema dragged up the corpse with great effort. He lighted a match and took a close look at the corpse. The rigid corpse stood up in the grave in front of him and Bheema groped all over the body. He found a ring on one of the fingers and pocketed it. He tore off the gold rings in the ears and then he remembered that there could be some gold in the mouth of the corpse. He pushed his fingers into the mouth but the jaws were locked tightly and he had to use his crowbar as a wedge to open the mouth. He opened it wide and put his fingers inside. At that very moment the pack of jackals set up a howl and scampered away into the jungle. At the sound the village dogs began to bark loudly, which awakened the people. Bheema could distinctly hear the call given by them to come together and drive away the jackals from the burial ground. This sent down a shiver of fear through his body. He found a ring in the mouth and put it into his pocket. To make a thorough search of the mouth cavity he put two fingers of his left hand into the mouth but found nothing. Inadvertently, he pulled out the iron bar before taking out his fingers.

The jaws shut together with a snap and his fingers were caught in a vice-like grip. A surging wave of excruciating pain passed through Bheema's body.

He saw people coming towards the burial ground, with lanterns in their hands. Fear grasped him and anger against the corpse welled up in him. In sheer rage he hit its skull with his crowbar. The impact of this blow tightened the hold of the jawbones on his fingers. The teeth cut deeper into his finger bones. He knew that if people found him in the act of defiling the graveyard they would either kill him or hand him over to the police after a good thrashing. So this is what they call a ghost, he thought, looking at the corpse. In his anger he hit the corpse still harder, cursing the devil to let him go.

By now people had approached the cemetery. Bheema pushed the bar into the mouth of the corpse and pried it open. When there was an opening he pulled out his fingers a bit cautiously. They were cut into pieces and were hanging to the base by shreds of skin. He suffered intense pain. Holding the broken fingers somehow in his fist he bolted towards home.

When he reached home he had high fever. Seeing the state he was in, his wife and child started wailing.

His fingers had to be amputated. The surgeon declared that it was the only way to save him. On the very day that he lost his fingers he learnt that the quarry work would start again. That giant of a man called Bheema wept like a child. Those very fingers with which he smashed stone to smithereens were lost for the sake of gold from the graveyard.

Translated from Marathi by H.V.V. Shintre

DALIT PANTHERS (BOMBAY, 1973)

The Dalit Panthers was founded in Bombay in 1972. The militant group was inspired by the Black Panther Party of the United States, and it emerged to fill the vacuum created in dalit politics of Maharashtra with the Republican Party of India founded by Ambedkar splitting into many factions. The Dalit Panthers led to a renaissance in Marathi literature and arts. They advocated and practised radical politics outside the framework of both parliamentary and Marxist-Leninist politics, fusing Ambedkar, Phule and Marx. Crucially, the Dalit Panthers helped popularise the term 'dalit' to refer to untouchable communities. Their influence was strongly felt in Karnataka and many other states. This manifesto issued in 1973 combines the Ambedkarite spirit with a broader Marxist framework and heralds the rise of autonomous dalit perspective in post-independence India.

DALIT PANTHERS' MANIFESTO

Revolutionary Stand of the Panthers

Today we, the 'Dalit Panthers', complete one year of our existence. Because of its clear revolutionary position, the 'Panthers' is growing in strength despite the strong resistance faced by it from many sides. It is bound to grow because it has recognized the revolutionary nature and aspirations of the masses with whose smiles and tears it has been bound up since its inception. During last year, motivated attempts have been made, especially in the far corners of Maharashtra, to create misunderstandings about our members and our activities. Misconceptions about the objectives of the 'Panthers', about its commitment to total revolutionary and democratic struggles, and about its policies, are being spread. It has, therefore, become clearly necessary to put forward our position. Because 'Panthers' no longer represent an emotional outburst of the dalits. Instead its character has changed into that of a political organization. Dr Babasaheb Ambedkar always taught his followers to base their calculations about their political strategy on deep study of the political situation confronting them. It is necessary and indispensable for us to keep this ideal before us. Otherwise we might mistake the back of the tortoise for a rock, and may be drowned in no time.

The present Congress rule is essentially a continuation of the old Hindu feudalism, which kept the dalits deprived of power, wealth and status for thousands of years. Therefore, this Congress rule cannot bring about social change. Under the pressure of the masses it passed many laws but it cannot implement them. Because the entire state machinery is dominated by the feudal interests, the same hands who, for thousands of years, under religious sanctions, controlled all the wealth and power, today own most of the agricultural land, industry, economic resources and all other instruments of power, therefore, in spite of independence and the democratic set-ups the problems of the dalit remain unsolved. Untouchability has remained intact. It remains intact because the government did not do anything to eradicate it except passing some laws against it.

To eradicate untouchability, all the land will have to be redistributed. Age-old customs and scriptures will have to be destroyed and new ideas inculcated. The village organization, the social organization, peoples' attitudes—all these will have to be restructured to suit true democratic objectives. We must pay attention to the objective process of social development and make an historical analysis of the power that imprisons the dalit and which has succeeded in making him tie his own hands. The Hindu feudal rule can be a hundred times more ruthless today in oppressing the dalits than it was in the Muslim period or the British period. Because this Hindu feudal rule has in its hands all the arteries of production, bureaucracy, judiciary, army and police forces, in the shape of feudals, landlords, capitalists and religious leaders who stand behind and enable these instruments to thrive. Hence the problem of untouchability of the dalits is no more one of mere mental slavery. Untouchability is the most violent form of exploitation on the surface of the earth, which survives the ever-changing forms of the power structure. Today it is necessary to seek its soil, its root causes. If we understand them, we can definitely strike at the heart of this exploitation. The oppression of dalits still exists despite the lives and work of our two great leaders—Jotiba Phule and Babasaheb Ambedkar. It is not only alive, it is stronger. Hence, unless we understand and give shape to the revolutionary content latent in the downtrodden lives of Untouchables, not a single individual seeking a social revolution would be able to remain alive in India.

Truly speaking, the problem of dalits, or Scheduled Castes and Tribes, has become a broad problem; the dalit is no longer merely an untouchable outside the village walls and the scriptures. He is an untouchable, and he is a dalit, but he is also a worker, a landless labourer, a proletarian. And unless we strengthen this growing revolutionary unity of the many with all our efforts, our existence has no future. The dalit must accordingly accept the sections of masses, the other revolutionary forces as part of his own movement. Only then will he be able to fight his enemies effectively. If this does not take place, we shall be condemned to a condition worse than slavery. We must develop and help this consciousness ripen every year, every month, day, hour and every moment. Then alone shall we possess the right to be called human beings at all.

It was for this that Dr Ambedkar made us realize our humanity even in our state of beast-like exploitation. We should, to be successful, accept and understand a thing only after deep study, with a calm mind. We should not fall prey to slogans and outbursts. We must uproot the varna system, the caste system that enslaves us in its snares. The soil in which they survive and grow must be made infertile. We must understand that the caste nature of the term dalit is breaking down.

What has the Government Done for the Dalits?

When India obtained independence in 1947, the face of the administrative class changed. In the place of the king came the president. In the place of the king's prime minister came the 'people's representative'. In the place of the Vedas, Upanishads, Manusmriti and Gita, came the Constitution. On a blank page, independence, equality, brotherhood proliferated. From 1947 to 1974 is a long period of time. In these twenty-seven years the Congress government, turning the electoral process into its own capital, has been ruling with a monopoly. Four five-year plans, five general elections and three wars have gone by in this post-independence 'coming of age'. But the problems and needs of the dalits, of the entire population, have been kept in a sort of deep freeze by the government. Beyond preserving state power in its hands, the government has done nothing else. On the contrary, by raising slogans of people's rule, of socialism, 'garibi hatao' (eliminate poverty) and green revolution, it has crushed the dalits, the landless, poor peasants and the working class under its feet. Gambling with their lives, tempting a handful amongst them, the government tried persistently to endanger their very existence. Using divisive tactics that split people along religious, caste and other lines, they endangered the very integrity of democracy.

In a democracy where men cannot exercise self-respect, well-being and an importance to their lives, where man cannot develop his individuality and his society, where those who wet with their blood every grain of the country's soil have to starve, where men have to forgo the land under their feet, the roof over their heads, where the upright have to break down and fall, where men have to see their mothers and sisters raped, in such a democracy, independence cannot be called true independence. The struggle for independence was a struggle under the leadership of national capitalists, landlords, feudals, for their own benefit. It was not under the leadership of the people, or of the dalits. And Dr Ambedkar had always said that it should be of the latter. That man called Gandhi, in whose hands the leadership of the struggle rested, was deceitful, cunning, an orthodox casteist and one who gave shelter to those who wanted to preserve class rule. Merely to preserve the unity of the independence struggle, he flirted with problems of the dalits, of untouchability, of the people. And that is why Babasaheb called him, time and again, the enemy of the people, the villain of the nation.

Babasaheb used to say, Gandhism means preservation of religious authority, Gandhism means traditionalism, Gandhism means casteism, Gandhism means preservation of traditional divisions of labour, Gandhism means incarnationism, Gandhism means the holy cow. Gandhism means worship of images, Gandhism means an unscientific outlook.

The British gave up their rule because of the seamen's mutiny, the emergence of the Azad Hind army, because of the struggles of the peasants, workers and dalits. Because of these they could no longer remain in power. Giving independence to Gandhi and Gandhians meant that the British wanted their own interests in the country to be looked after. This was the sort of borrowed independence we got. True independence is one that is snatched forcibly out of the hands of the enemy. One that is like bits thrown to a helpless beggar is no independence. In every house and every mind the flame of true independence has to be ignited. This did not happen. That is why the dalit, the worker, the landless and the poor peasant did not become free, the muck at the bottom of the pond remained where it was and, in fact, the government that retained the status quo kept on telling bigger and bigger lies to the dalits.

What have Other Parties Done for the Dalits?
The Left parties, having fought five elections, have grown bankrupt. They are now interested in moving from elections to elections. In 1967 the Left parties united against the Congress. There was such opportunism in the united front that parties like the Communists joined hands with communalist parties such as Jan Sangh and Muslim League. In some states, Left united fronts came to power. But the absence of a clear-cut programme made the anti-Congress stand useless. In the task of putting some alternatives before the people, of solving the problems of the dalits, of establishing the rule of the poor in the country', all the Left parties proved powerless. As a result, revolutionary people's groups lost faith in electoral democracy. Uprisings like Naxalbari took place and the spark spread around the country. With the 1972 elections, things came back to square one.

The Congress sat like a beast on the head of the dalits, of the people; famine struck, the very livelihoods of crores of people were uprooted, animals perished. Factories were shut down, workers faced unemployment, everyone was harassed by the mounting price rise. The full eclipse that Congress rule represents for the life of the country has not yet terminated. But our Left parties, playing the politics of parliamentary seats, are still wasting time trying to get recognition from the Congress. Not one dares to turn revolutionary to take up the problems of the people. All those Left parties who do not possess political power have ignored questions of a social revolution. They have not combined the class struggle with the struggle against untouchability, have not raised a voice against cultural and social domination along with economic exploitation. Untouchability is nothing but an extremely poisonous sort of exploitation. This exploitative system was given birth by Hindu feudalism and thrives for its benefit.

The framework of untouchability is simply widening with the help of the army, the prisons, the legal system and the bureaucracy. Under the name of high-flown philosophy and liberation of the soul (moksha, nirvana), dalits have been deprived of earthly happiness, and have been looted of all they possess. With the industrial revolution, machines came into being. Dalits were harnessed to the machines. But in the minds of the upper castes, feudalism survived. Because the owners of the machines could make a profit only by keeping the social structure intact. Only if a social revolution grips the minds of the dalits, will there be a political revolution. If this takes place, the upper caste, the upper class, will lose the power it possesses. The stand that is taken by the Left parties prevents the spread of revolutionary ideology amongst the people. Because struggles really and truly meaningful to the dalits were not conducted, dalits have grown poorer. They have had to face innumerable atrocities.

The Republican Party and Dalit Panthers
The problems of the dalits today, be they social, political or ethical, cannot be solved within the framework of religion and caste. This is what Dr Babasaheb realized after his defeat in the 1952 general elections. A scientific outlook, class consciousness and a completely atheistic and fighting humanism alone could add an edge to the struggles of the dalits. For this purpose, Dr Ambedkar wanted to transfer the then-existing Scheduled Caste Federation (SCF) into a broad-based party. This could not happen during his lifetime. After his death, his

'followers' simply renamed SCF as the Republican Party and started to pursue casteist politics. They never united all the dalits and all the oppressed. Above all, they conducted the politics of a revolutionary community like the dalits in a legalistic manner. The party got enmeshed in the web of votes, demands, select places for a handful of the dalits and concessions. So the dalit population scattered over the country, in many villages, remained politically where they were. The leadership of the party went into the hands of the middle class in the community.

Intrigue, selfishness and division became rife. Destroying the revolutionary voice of Dr Ambedkar, these contemptible leaders made capital out of his name and set up their beggars' bowls. This is Dr Ambedkar's party, they said. This is Dr Ambedkar's flag, they said, and filled their coffers. And thus, except the satyagraha of the landless conducted under Dadasaheb Gaekwad's leadership, the party did not take up any programme worth its name. The atrocities against dalits grew endemic. In a period of one to one and a half years, 1,117 dalits were murdered. The land grew barren, not a drop of water was available. Honour was violated, houses gutted, people killed. Along with the very question of living, physical indignities grew sharper. What did the Republican Party do? The party got caught in the net cast by a cunning ruling-class leader like Yashwantrao Chavan. Its life perished. Unity vanished, impotents filled the party. If we put our future in the hands of such impotent leaders, we will forgo our very lives, and that is why today we have to announce with deep pain that we are no blood relatives of the Republican Party.

The Dalits (Oppressed) of the World and Panthers

Due to the hideous plot of American imperialism, the Third Dalit World, that is, oppressed nations, and dalit people are suffering. Even in America, a handful of reactionary whites are exploiting Negroes. To meet the force of reaction and remove this exploitation, the Black Panther movement grew. From the Black Panthers, Black Power emerged. The fire of the struggles has thrown out sparks into the country. We claim a close relationship with this struggle. We have before our eyes the examples of Vietnam, Cambodia, Africa and the like.

Who is a Dalit?

Members of Scheduled Castes and Tribes, neo-Buddhists, the working people, the landless and poor peasants, women and all those who are being exploited politically, economically and in the name of religion.

Who are our Friends?

1. Revolutionary parties set to break down the caste system and class rule. Left parties that are Left in a true sense.
2. All other sections of society that are suffering due to the economic and political oppression.

Who are our Enemies?

1. Power, wealth, price.
2. Landlords, capitalists, moneylenders and their lackeys.
3. Those parties who indulge in religious or casteist politics, and the government, which depends on them.

Burning Questions before Dalits Today

1. Food, clothing, shelter.
2. Employment, land, (removal of) untouchability.
3. Social and physical injustice.

The struggle for the emancipation of the dalits needs a complete revolution. Partial change is impossible. We do not want it either. We want a complete and total revolutionary change. Even if we want to move out of the present state of social degradation alone, we will have to exercise our power in economic, political, cultural fields as well. We will not be satisfied easily now. We do not want a little place in the Brahman Alley. We want the rule of the whole lane. We are not looking at persons but at a system. Change of heart, liberal education, etc. will not end our state of exploitation. When we gather a revolutionary mass, rouse the people, out of the struggle of this giant mass will come the tidal wave of revolution. Legalistic appeals, requests, demands for concessions, elections, satyagraha—out of these, society will never change. Our ideas of social revolution and rebellion will not be borne by such paper-made vehicles. They will sprout in the soil, flower in the mind and then will come into full being with the help of a steel-strong vehicle.

Dalit Panther is not a Mere Slogan

The way we look at our questions is the first step to solving them. The Panthers will paralyzingly attack untouchability, casteism and economic exploitation. This social system and state have taken many a cruel path to convert us into slaves. Turned us long into 'shudras'. In the present modern forms of slavery there are mental chains of slavishness. We will try to break them. In our struggle we will become free.

Our Programme

1. More than 80 percent of India's population lives in the villages. Of these, landless peasants are 35 percent and 33 percent of all landless agricultural labourers belong to Scheduled Castes. (Those dalit poor peasants who own pieces of land, own a negligible amount.) The question of landlessness of the dalit peasants must be resolved.

2. Feudal survivals are still to be found in the villages. Due to this, dalits are cruelly oppressed and exploited. Landlords and rich peasants get social prestige along with wealth. Due to this, the atrocities on the dalits have grown endemic. This system has clamped itself on the dalit's chest, affecting every part of his life, from day-to-day living to the deeper economic questions. This system must be destroyed.

3. Landless peasants must immediately get excess land through the application of the land ceiling act. Waste and jungle land must likewise be distributed.

4. The wages of landless labourers must be increased.

5. Dalits must be allowed to draw water from public wells.

6. Dalits must live, not outside the village in a separate settlement, but in the village itself.

7. All means of production must belong to the dalits.

8. Exploitation by private capital must cease. Foreign capital must be confiscated without compensation.

9. Social, cultural and economic exploitation must be removed and socialism must he built in India. Misleading nationaliza-

tion must give way to a true introduction of socialism.

10. All dalits must be assured of daily wages.

11. Unemployed dalits must be given unemployment benefits.

12. All dalits must be given free education, medical facilities, housing and good quality cheap grains.

13. When giving employment in educational institutions, the requirement to declare one's caste and religion must be immediately removed.

14. The government must stop giving grants to religious institutions immediately and the wealth of religious places must be used for the benefit of dalits.

15. Religious and casteist literature must be banned.

16. The division in the army along caste lines must be ended.

17. Black-marketeers, hoarders, moneylenders and all those exploiting the people economically must be destroyed.

18. The prices of essential commodities must be reduced.

We will build the organization of workers, dalits, landless, poor peasants through all city factories, in all villages. We will hit back against all injustice perpetrated on dalits. We will well and truly destroy the caste and varna system that thrives on the people's misery, which exploits the people, and liberate the dalits. The present legal system and state have turned all our dreams to dust. To eradicate all the injustice against dalits, they must themselves become rulers. This is the people's democracy. Sympathizers and members of Dalit Panthers, be ready for the final struggle of the dalits!

K. SATYANARAYANA AND SUSIE THARU

INTRODUCTION: KERALA [DALIT LITERATURE]

The contemporary dalit movement in Kerala is marked by small group initiatives in the intellectual domain, the recovery of important historical figures, struggles for equality in the church and mass mobilization against land alienation and against oppression of adivasis and dalits. "The dalit movement is a broad democratic movement today," observes the critic, K.K. Baburaj. The movement was enabled by the availability of Ambedkar's writings in translation, the reassessment of the Kerala renaissance[1] and the rejection of mainstream economic interpretations of Kerala society. Together, these led to the positioning of caste as a question of democracy.

Dalit assertion in Kerala can be divided into two broad phases: the activities of the SEEDIAN (Socially, Economically, Educationally Depressed Indian Ancient Natives) group and dalit Christian movements beginning in the 1980s and, in the 1990s and after, the activities around the Dalit Women's Society, Dalit Students Forum, the Adivasi Gothra Mahasabha and a substantial amount of intellectual and creative work by activists, writers and painters as well as academics working in universities.

The 1970s and 1980s

In the 1970s, SEEDIAN tried to develop a new theoretical perspective for India, drawing on Marxism and Ambedkarism.[2] The group comprised K.K. Kochu, Baburaj, K.K.S. Das, K.K.S. Ambirajan, N.K. Kamalasanan, Paul Chirakkarodu, V.V. Swamy, Sunny Kapikkad and others. Many of them had been associated with the Left and were

---

[1] The Kerala Renaissance refers to early-twentieth-century movements of socio-religious reform, most importantly that of Sree Narayana Guru who campaigned against the caste system, brahmin supremacy and many social disabilities. Dalits today point out that these movements did not address the dalit question.

[2] This section is based on interviews with the SEEDIAN group.

interested in reinterpreting Marxism in the context of caste in India. SEEDIAN represented the initial break from the ML movement and later from Marxism itself, notes Sunny Kapikkad. The group produced the journal SEEDIAN and brought out 'November Books', which was an initiative to study history as a team and introduce thinkers such as Antonio Gramsci, Mao Tse-tung, Gabriel Garcia Marquez, D.D. Kosambi, Bertrand Russell and a number of African writers and thinkers to Malayalam readers.

In 1991, around the time of the pro- and anti-Mandal discussions at the national level, the SEEDIAN group broke up over differences, principally over the issue of participating in elections. Maoist groups had generally boycotted elections and called for a 'new democratic revolution', while Kochu and others argued that dalits should participate. The shift from theorizing a long-term agrarian evolution to democratization in present-day Kerala society can be mapped through the SEEDIAN debates.

After the breakup of SEEDIAN, the independent journal *Soochakam* was started by a smaller group. It provided space to interrogate the given categories of hegemonic power and carried debates on the formulation of the agrarian revolution, criticizing the class-based idea of the New Democratic Revolution. It also documented the ongoing discussions on democratization. A new publication venture, Subject and Language Press, has also been started to carry forward these early initiatives in articulating not only the dalit question but, more broadly, that of democracy in India.

Dalit Christian movement

The 'Separate Administration' movement (1960–66), initiated by Vattappara John Stephen, challenged the upper-caste power structure of the Syrian Christians and demanded a representative leadership for dalits in the church.[3] In the 1970s and early 1980s the dalit question emerged again, for the first time after the missionary moment of the

---

[3] Conversations with Yesudasan on the dalit Christian movements helped immensely. See also his book-length study, *Baliyaadukalude Vamshaavali* (Genealogy of the Scapegoats), which examines the history, politics and implications of dalit accession to Protestant Christianity in central Kerala. This was named one of the ten best books of 2010 by *India Today* (Malayalam).

nineteenth century, as one of the key public questions in the Church of South India (CSI). The demands of the movement included proportional representation for dalits in jobs in church-controlled schools, colleges and hospitals, and opportunities and power in the church and its various bodies.

T.M. Yesudasan played a key role in the CSI Youth Movement, which raised the caste question; the movement also linked up with activists whose work among the fisher-people, the tribals and the poor had been inspired by the liberation theology movements in Latin America. They held discussions and organized meetings and lectures. Recollecting that time, Yesudasan observes, "A large number of important [world] thinkers of that time visited Kerala at our invitation."

A padayathra was organized by the movement in the late 1980s to push the issue into the public arena and open the discussion in remote areas. Wide recognition for the movement after the padayathra disturbed the administration; the church diocesan council meeting turned into a battlefield. While acknowledging what the early Christian missionaries had done for dalits, there was also criticism against them as they gave English education to the Syrian Christians and vernacular education to dalits. Yesudasan critiques traditional history's neglect of the history of dalit slavery and the event of conversion, and argues that the grass-roots movements that emerged against these backdrops contribute to the democratization of Kerala society.

Through groups such as the Janakeeya Vimochana Viswasaprasthanam and Dynamic Action, a number of issues, including that of land rights, were taken up. Activists collected, interpreted and sang folk songs, produced plays and spoke of a Black God and the calling to be a Church of the Poor. "When our group presented the folk songs," activist M.J. Joseph recalls, "something lost was clearly being awakened ... the spiritual link between dalit life and the land, the production process..." The dalit singer C.J. Kuttappan speaks about the songs as "not human centred, but life centred" and respecting, in their rhythms and themes, a "mannu marayada—decorum of the earth". "We are an agricultural people," he says, "and it is these rhythms that wake the earth, sky, birds and trees, that will bring us together." In two historically significant little magazines, *Yuvalokam* (1983–) and *Dynamic Action* (1988–89), it was argued that the Church of South India had to acknowledge that it was actually built up by dalit Christians who constituted its real calling and the overwhelming majority of its membership.

Activists also began to speak of slavery as an important aspect of the dalit experience—and of the Christian church in Kerala. New interest was kindled in organizations such as the Prathyaksha Raksha Daiva Sabha (PRDS) that had kept alive dalit memories of slavery and had in fact shaped a theology and ritual practice around that issue.

New forums and campaigns

Several other small forums were set up and mass campaigns taken up in Kerala in the 1990s.[4]

Among them were the Adhasthitha Navodhana Munnani or Movement for the Renaissance of the Depressed (1985–92)—led by K.M. Salimkumar—the Kerala Dalit Panthers, a militant group based in Kollam, and the Indian Dalit Federation (IDF) formed by Paul Chirakkarodu. The IDF organized the Guruvayur Padayathra across Kerala to gain access to the ootupura in the famous temple where, even in 2010, untouchables and non-Hindus are not allowed entry. The Sree Narayana Dharma Paripalanayogam (SNDP) supported the campaign. The IDF later merged into the Bahujan Samaj Party.

A number of the leading dalit intellectuals in Kerala today were at some point members of the lively student discussion group in Kurichi mentored by Lovely Stephen and T.M. Yesudasan. Lovely was also one of the founding members of the Dalit Women's Society (DWS), which came into being in Kurichi in 1992. Academics and thinkers were roped into the group, which also sought out young talent. They read Ambedkar, political and cultural theory from all over the world and critically analyzed different formations in Kerala society: the CPM-initiated land reforms, Kerala history and mainstream Malayalam culture and literature. Critiques of the world-famous Kerala model of

---

[4] Interviews with Paul Chirakkarodu, Yesudasan, Sunny Kapikkad, M.B. Manoj, M.R. Renukumar, Rekharaj and Sanal Mohan, among others, provided us insights into the dalit cultural and political assertion of the 1990s.

development found their early formulations in this context, as also the influential critique and reassessment of Malayalam literature that appeared in a special issue of the mainstream journal *Bhashaposhini*, in 1997, and in the Sahitya Akademi journal, *Sahitya Lokam* (July–August 1998). It was argued that the political community in Kerala was structured to exclude dalits. Short story writer C. Ayyappan reports that though his first book had come out in 1986, it was only fourteen years later that it received serious critical attention in a *Bhashaposhini* article. The Kurichi group also produced a play based on Ayyappan's story *Pretha Bhashanam* (Ghost Speech). Painter and poet Renukumar notes that the discussions in the Kurichi student group enabled them to articulate a mature argument, capable of countering that of the dominant political culture in Kerala.

A Centre for Kerala Dalit Studies was set up to advance the theoretical debate around dalit issues. In 2000 the Kurichi Samara Sahaya Samithi was formed with the involvement of Geethanandan, K. Appukuttan, M.D. Thomas, Sunny Kapikkad, M.B. Manoj, Renukumar, Rekharaj and others. They were overwhelmed by the huge public response, mainly from dalits, which they received on the protests organized against the 11 kV high-tension wire that was to pass over the Kurichi dalit colony. It was clear that there was a constituency waiting for these issues to be articulated. The Samithi became active in a number of strikes and agitations. The Dalit Sahitya Vedy (Dalit Literary Forum) was formed in 1991. V.V. Swamy, who was active in setting it up, was keen to reopen the discussion on the PRDS and in 1999 he played an important role in the creation of two intellectual forums, the PRDS Seminar Sanghadaka Samithi and the PRDS Samskarika Vedi.

Malayalam literature was a key area of work. During this period, nineteenth-century giants such as Potheri Kunjambu were rediscovered and dalit readings produced of Mrs Collins' *Ghathakavadham* (*The Slayer Slain*, 1877). Critics identify three periods in Malayalam dalit literature.[5] In the first period, the focus is on slavery, where con-

---

[5] George K. Alex and Elizabeth John, ed., *Reinventing Identity: An Anthology of Dalit Writers from Kerala* (Mumbai: Vikas Adhyayan Kendra, 2008), 19.

version to Christianity was seen as a solution; in the second period, after a century-long hiatus, writers like T.K.C. Vaduthala (1921–88), Kallada Sasi, Kallara Sukumaran and Kaviyoor Murali emerge. The term 'dalit' was not in use at the time, but the critic M. Dasan writes that Vaduthala's work was a "celebration of Pulaya life and culture with all its good and bad aspects. It also portrays dalit rituals, beliefs, ceremonies and superstitions."[6] Most of these writers were close to Marxist parties, rejected conversion as a solution and called for change of political ideology. It is in the third 'dalit' phase that there is a real flowering of literary activity, in which the specificity of caste is explored as a form of privilege that finds new life in modern institutions. This phase is represented by poets, short story writers and critics such as Paul Chirakkarodu, C. Ayyappan, T.H.P Chentharassery, T.M. Yesudasan, K.K. Kochu, Sunny Kapikkad, S. Joseph and M.R. Renukumar.

The largest and most significant struggle taken up was that of the adivasis over land, and radical dalit groups supported this struggle. Kapikkad and other dalit leaders actively participated in the forty-eight-day-long struggle of the adivasis led by C.K. Janu and Geethanandan in 2001, and again in the Muthanga protests of 2003 and the Chengara struggle in 2009.

In Kerala, as in Tamil Nadu, Babasaheb Ambedkar's birth centenary in 1991 acted as a catalyst to make dalit intellectual and activist writings visible in the public sphere.[7] Speaking of the impact of this moment, Kapikkad says: "Before the 1990s we thought of Ambedkar as a forerunner of Marxism, and spoke of Marx and Ambedkar. After the 1990s we realized that Marxism was not suitable for an analysis of Indian society. Caste was not a behaviour pattern that could be set aside; it was social, economic and cultural capital [soththu adhikaram]."

---

[6] M. Dasan, "Validating the Voice of the Avarnas: A Study of Vaduthala's Caste Stories," *Calicut University Research Journal* 3 (2002), 58.

[7] Dasan mentions small journals such as *Uparodham* edited by the late Cherayi Ramadas, *Pithrubhumi* edited by N.R. Santhosh and publication units like Kerala Dalit Sahitya Academy, *Dalithakam* and *Pedabhetham* that published dalit literature. See Dasan, "Validating the Voice of the Avarnas," 55.

KUMUD PAWDE

Born into a mahar family in Nagpur, Maharashtra, Kumud Somkuvar (1938–) chose to study and then teach Sanskrit defying two-fold discrimination on grounds of gender and caste. She married Motiram Pawde, a social worker of the kunbi maratha caste and became Kumud Pawde. Her work Antasphot *('Outburst', 1981)—from which this excerpt is taken—was the first published autobiography by a dalit woman. She is professor of Sanskrit and the president of the All India Progressive Women's Organisation.*

THE STORY OF MY 'SANSKRIT'

A lot of things are often said about me to my face. I've grown used to listening to them quietly; it's become a habit. What I have to listen to is praise. Actually, I don't at all like listening to praise. You may say that this itself is a form of self-indulgence. But that isn't so. I mean it sincerely. When I hear myself praised, it's like being stung by a lot of gadflies. As a result, I look askance at the person praising me. This expression must look like annoyance at being praised, for many misunderstandings have arisen about me in this connection. But it can't be helped. My acquaintances get angry with me because I am unable to accept compliments gracefully. I appear ill-mannered to them, because there isn't in me the courtesy they are expecting.

Now if you want to know why I am praised—well, it's for my knowledge of Sanskrit, my ability to learn it and to teach it. Doesn't anyone ever learn Sanskrit? That's not the point. The point is that Sanskrit and the social group I come from, don't go together in the Indian mind. Against the background of my caste, the Sanskrit I have learned appears shockingly strange.

That a woman from a caste that is the lowest of the low should learn Sanskrit, and not only that, also teach it—is a dreadful anomaly to a traditional mind. And an individual in whose personality these anomalies are accumulated becomes an object of attraction—an attraction blended of mixed acceptance and rejection. The attraction based on acceptance comes from my caste-fellows, in the admiration of whose glance is pride in an impossible achievement. That which for so many centuries was not to be touched by us, is now within our grasp. That which remained encased in the shell of difficulty, is now accessible. Seeing this knowledge hidden in the esoteric inner sanctum come within the embrace, not just of any person, but one whom religion has considered to be vermin—that is their victory.

The other attraction—based on rejection—is devastating. It pricks holes in one's mind—turning a sensitive heart into a sieve. Words of praise of this kind, for someone who is aware, are like hot spears. It is fulsome praise. Words that come out from lips' edge as filthy as betel-stained spit. Each word gleaming smooth as cream. Made up of the fragility of a honey-filled shirish blossom. Polished as marble. The sensation is that of walking on a soft velvety carpet—but being burnt by the hot embers hidden in someone's breast, and feeling the scorching pain in one's soul. The one who's speaking thinks the listener can't understand—for surely a low-caste person hasn't the ability to comprehend. But some people intend to be understood, so that I'll be crushed by the words. "Well, isn't that amazing! So you're teaching Sanskrit at the Government College, are you? That's very gratifying, I must say." The words are quite ordinary; their literal meaning is straight-forward. But the meaning conveyed by the tone in which they are said torments me in many different ways! "In what former life have I committed a sin that I should have to learn Sanskrit even from you?" "All our sacred scriptures have been polluted." Some despair is also conveyed by their facial expressions. "It's all over! Kaliyug has dawned. After all, they're the government's favourite sons-in-law! We have to accept it all."

There are some other people I know, who have a genuine regard for me. They are honestly amazed by how I talk, by my clean, clear pronunciation. They speak with affectionate admiration about my mode of living. The food I cook is equated with ambrosia. They detect a brahminical standard of culture in my every thought and action—enough to surprise them. They constantly try to reconcile the contradiction. It's my good luck that I'm not always being asked to account for my antecedents, like Satyakam Jabali. The main point is that they are trying to understand my evident good breeding in the context of my caste, and that is what makes everything so novel for them.

The result is that although I try to forget my caste, it is impossible to forget. And then I remember an expression I heard somewhere: 'What comes by birth, but can't be cast off by dying—that is caste.'

Beyond the accepters and the rejecters lies yet another group. In wholeheartedly welcoming the admiration of this group, every corner of my being is filled with pleasure. This group consists of my students. Far removed from hostile feelings. Without even an iota of caste consciousness. Away from the prejudices of their elders. Pure, innocent admiration, prompted by the boundless respect they feel, fills their eyes. Actually these girls have reached the age of understanding. The opinions they hear around them should by rights have made an impression on their mind. But these precious girls are full to the brim with the ability to discriminate impartially. And they keep their admiration within the limits of their gaze; they do not allow it to reach their lips. And that's why I yearn for that admiration. The occasional forward girl who has suppressed her timidity makes bold to express her feelings. "Madam, I wish your lesson would never end!" And I answer her woodenly: "But the college doesn't feel that way." She feels snubbed, but I don't wish to encourage her admiration, in case it becomes a habit.

If the admiration had stayed limited to this individual level, I would tolerate it, but it goes beyond the prescribed boundaries. In other words, it starts to be blazoned even at the official level. As usual they start beating the drum of my caste, and tunes of praise of my knowledge of Sanskrit begin to mingle with the drumbeat. On the Vijaya Dashami day of 1971, the Maharashtra State Government arranged, at Nagpur, a felicitation meeting to honour scholars of the Vedas. According to the wishes of the Honourable ex-Minister of Education, Shri Madhukarrao Chaudhary, I was to introduce these honoured scholars. Of course the inspiration was that of Dr Kolte. The introduction was to be made in Sanskrit. "In the times of the Aryans it was noted down, and moreover impressed on the minds of the common Indian people, from the Himalayas to the tip of the peninsula, that my ancestors should consider themselves guilty of a crime if they even heard the sound of this language. And that is the language in which I have to speak." My god! How was I going to manage? My heart began to beat rapidly. My mind was dark with anxiety, and I was drowned in feelings of inferiority. A conflict of emotions—and once again a confrontation with public praise. "Whereas our traditional books have forbidden the study of Sanskrit by women and shudras, a woman from those very shudras, from the lowest caste among them, will today, in Sanskrit, introduce these scholars. This is the beginning of a progressive way of thinking in independent India." A thunder of applause. I look towards the sound of the applause. Most of the people here are from government offices. Looking at them through an artist's eyes, I see what looks like a wild disco-dance of different emotions. The frustration of the defeated, the fury of the traditionalists, the respect of some acquaintances, the hostility and disgust of others, are obvious to my experienced eye. Some gazes ask me, "Why did you need to make the introductions in this manner? To humiliate us?"

In response to these hissings of wounded pride, I experience a mixture of emotions. Seeing this hostility and disgust, I slip into the past. This disgust is extremely familiar to me. In fact, that is what I have grown accustomed to, ever since I was old enough to understand. Actually, I shouldn't have any feelings about this disgust, and if I do have any feelings at all they should be of gratitude. For it was this disgust that inclined me towards Sanskrit. It so happened that the ghetto in which there stood my place of birth, the house where I was welcome, was encircled on all sides by the houses of caste Hindus. The people in our ghetto referred to them as the Splendid People. A small girl like me, seven or eight years old, could not understand why they called them 'splendid'. And even as today's mature female with learning from innumerable books, I still cannot understand it. That is,

I have understood the literal meaning of the word 'splendid'. But not why it should be applied to them, or whether they deserve to have it applied. The girls who studied along with me were brahmins or from other higher castes. I had to pass their houses. I paused, waiting casually for their company. Right in front of me, the mothers would warn their daughters, "Be careful! Don't touch her. Stay away from her. And don't play with her. Or I won't let you into the house again." Those so-called educated, civilized mothers were probably unconscious of the effect of this on my young mind. It wasn't as if I could not understand them.

Every day, I bathed myself clean with Pears soap. My mother rubbed Kaminia oil on my hair, and plaited it neatly. My clothes were well-washed and sparkling clean. The girls of my own caste liked to play with me because it enabled them to smell some fragrance. For my father himself was fond of toiletries. So there was always a variety of oils, soaps and perfumes in the house. The other girls in my class (except for those who lived near my ghetto) also liked to sit next to me. So why should these women have talked like that?

What's more, if one were to compare houses, our house was cleaner than theirs. My mother daily smeared the floor with fresh cowdung. The white-powder borders were delicately drawn. The courtyard was well-sprinkled, and decorated with rangoli designs. Almost every fortnight, on the occasion of a festival, the house was whitewashed from top to bottom. Every scrap of cloth was boiled in a solution of soda bicarb before it was washed. The metal vessels were scrubbed to gleam. On the other hand, one could see water stains and a greasy film on even the drinking-vessels those girls had. In fact, it was I who didn't like to sit next to those girls. For, from my childhood, my sense-organs had been sharp and vigorous. My sense of smell, in particular, had sharpened beyond limit. Though, of course, the nose that conveyed it was broad and misshapen. The sour smell, like buttermilk, that rose from the bodies of those girls! I couldn't bear the smell of shikakai mixed with the smell of their hair. Their bad breath, too, was unbearable. And, in spite of all this, they found me disgusting? So, even at that young age, this emotion of disgust taught me to think. It inspired me to be introspective. At an age which was meant for playing and skipping around, these thoughts would rouse me to fury.

One event outraged my self-respect. There was to be a thread-ceremony for the brother of one of my classmates. I had not actually been invited but my restless curiosity would not let me sit quiet. I stood outside the pandal looking in at the ceremony going on inside. The sacrificial fire was lit; the air all around was filled with the smoke and fragrance of incense and the grain burnt-offering. The reverberations of the Vedic chants threatened to burst through the cloth walls of the pandal. I was lost in watching the head-movements that accompanied the chant of "Svaha!" each time a libation was poured. All this was extremely new, unknown, never seen before. I was totally engrossed, at one with the chants and the incense.

My concentration was suddenly broken. One voice: "Hey, girl! What are you staring at? Can you make head or tail of it? Here, take a laddoo—and be off!" A decked-up woman past her prime, dripping with gold and pearls, stood in front of me, adjusting the pallav of her heavily-brocaded sari. Her nose was wrinkled in disgust, like a shrivelled fig. "What do you take me for—a beggar? Giving me a laddoo! Can you see injuries on anyone just because I watched them?" I retorted, and briskly walked away.

Words followed me: "These mahars have really got above themselves." The intonation was the typical superior nasal tone of the Pune brahmin.

My young mind thought, "Why was I so wrapped up in watching? What had that ceremony to do with me? And why should that woman behave so bitchily with me?" There was definitely some intimate connection between me and those Vedic mantras. Otherwise why should that woman have noticed my innocent absorption? Why should she have taunted me disgustedly? She must have been unwilling to let those chants enter my ears. I used to ask my father, "What language are the Vedic mantras composed in?" He used to say, "They're in Sanskrit, my girl." "Is Sanskrit very difficult? Can't we learn it?" My father used to answer, "Why shouldn't we? After all, we're independent now. Those days are gone. Learn Sanskrit. Don't I too know the Gayatri mantra?" And he used to say "Om" and begin to recite the Gayatri mantra. In simple delight, I used to tell my neighbours, "I'm going to learn Sanskrit." The educated people next door used to poke fun at me. "Is Sanskrit such an easy language? It's very difficult. Did our forefathers ever learn it?" Hearing this, I would be discouraged. Seeing my crestfallen face, my father would start cursing those people, sometimes obscenely, sometimes more elegantly. He used to encourage me, and the encouragement would make me glow with confidence once again.

After I entered high school, I took Sanskrit as an elective subject in class nine. The school where I went supported brahminical prejudices. All sorts of indirect efforts were systematically made to prevent me from learning Sanskrit. "You won't be able to manage. There will be no one at home to help you. Sanskrit is very difficult," etc. But I was as firm as a rock. Seeing that no form of persuasion had any effect on me, the persuaders stopped persuading. But how to remove the prejudice in their minds? I did not want to pay heed to every single opinion. I just wanted to keep my teacher, Hatekar, happy. He had been full of praise of me since I was in class six. "How can this little slip of a girl give answers so fast in every subject?" I asked him, "Sir, I should take Sanskrit, shouldn't I?" "Do take it. But you've taken all the Arts subjects, though you're good at math. Take science and math, along with Sanskrit." "But sir, I don't enjoy math." "But you can become a doctor, can't you?" "I don't want to be a doctor. I can't bear suffering." He laughed and said, "On the contrary, it is precisely those who can't bear suffering, who are fit to become doctors. Won't you be able to help the afflicted? That's what's needed among your people. But it's your decision."

With great eagerness and interest, I began my study of Sanskrit. As I learnt the first-declension masculine form of the word 'deva', I picked up the rhythm of the chant. I must make special mention of the person who helped me to learn by rote the first lesson about aspirates—my teacher Gokhale. If I omit to do so, I shall feel a twinge of disloyalty in every drop of my blood. Gokhale Guruji. Dhoti, long-sleeved shirt, black cap, a sandalwood-paste mark on his forehead. The typical robust and clear pronunciation of the Vedic school. And an incredible concern for getting his students to learn Sanskrit. At first I was afraid. But this proved groundless. What actually happened was the very opposite of what I had expected.

I had been sent by the Bhide Kanya Shala to take part in some essay competition or the other. The centre for the competition was the Bhonsale Vedic School. No part of the Mahal area was familiar to me. I timidly explained my difficulty, to Gokhale Guruji. He said, "Why don't you come to my house? (He never addressed us in the second person singular; it was always a respectful plural.) I'll take you along." And he gave me his address. I reached the address asking for directions repeatedly in the lanes and alleys of the Mahal area. My teacher's house was in fact a sprawling mansion. A huge, well-swept courtyard with a tulsi vrindavan and a well, and a small Shiva temple within it. All looked as antique as a well-preserved old Benares brocade. I hesitantly entered. "Welcome," he greeted me in friendly tones. Two boys, about ten or eleven years old, came out to see who had arrived. From their general appearance—the dhoti, shirt, top-knot and sandalwood mark, as well as their features—they appeared to be Guruji's children. After a while, on being called by Guruji, his wife came outside. She was dressed in silk for ritual purity. Her face brimmed with godliness. Every movement of her body was eloquent with hospitality. The formalities of introduction were completed. She hurried inside, and after a while, the older boy came out bearing plates full of cooked poha. I became nervous, fear crept over my mind. Suppose this lady were to find out my caste? Along with sips of water, I swallowed the lump in my throat as well as mouthfuls of poha. I couldn't concentrate on what anyone was saying. My only worry was when and how I could escape from there. Suppose someone from the Buldy area were to come there?

"God deliver me from this ordeal!" I kept praying to the almighty. But nothing terrible happened. For those people were indeed very kind. Open and relaxed in their conversation. My teacher, for one, definitely knew my caste. But I was not made to experience any feeling of inferiority. And I felt a profound respect for him. The broad-mind-edness of this brahmin incarnate, with his old-fashioned upbringing, remained constant even towards a student of the very lowest caste. Needless to say, it was evidence of his high thinking and his generous heart. It became my aim to study faithfully as my teacher instructed me and never to anger him by inattention to studies. You can never tell who will become a shining light to whose life. Guruji was prob-ably unaware that he had the power to add a touch of glory to the life of an insignificant being. After I matriculated, I did not meet him again. Perhaps he won't even recognize me. But I wish to lighten my load of respect by paying back a fraction of my sacred debt with the fee of words. For if Guruji had not shown me that warmth, but had instead shown the base feelings appropriate to his orthodox nature, would I have learnt Sanskrit?

Against all obstacles, I at last matriculated. On seeing the marks I got for Sanskrit, I announced, "I shall do an M.A. in Sanskrit." Our enlightened neighbours laughed as they had before. Some college lec-turers and lawyers also joined in the joke. "How can that be possible? You may have got good marks at matric. But it isn't so easy to do an M.A. in Sanskrit. You shouldn't make meaningless boasts; you should know your limitations." The discouragers said what they usually do. The point was that the people who discouraged me were all of my caste. But their words could not turn me from my purpose. I didn't reply—I wanted to answer them by action. For that, I needed to study very hard. In order to take an M.A. in Sanskrit, I would have to go to the famous Morris College. I had heard so many things about the col-lege from my friend's sister. About the learned professors with their cultivated tastes, about the mischievous male students, the beautiful girls, and the huge library. My interest was limited to the professors who would teach me, and to the library. And I joined the college.

The Hindus from the high-caste areas used to taunt me. "Even these wretched outcastes are giving themselves airs these days—stud-ying in colleges." I pretended to be deaf. I had begun to have some idea of what Savitribai Phule must have had to endure on account of her husband Mahatma Jotiba Phule's zeal for women's education.

I went through some mixed experiences while I studied. I would call my lecturers' even-handed fairness a very remarkable thing. I was never scared by the prejudice of which repute and rumour had told me. What is more, praise and encouragement were given according to merit. Some people may have felt dislike in their heart of hearts, but they never displayed it. One thing alone irked me—the ironical comments about the scholarship I got. "She's having fun and games at the expense of a scholarship. Just bloated with government money!" From the peons themselves to the senior officials, there was the same attitude. I couldn't understand. Was it charity they were dispensing from their personal coffers? They were giving me government money, and if that money was going from them to the government in the form of taxes, then equally, a tax was being levied on the public to pay their salaries. And that tax was collected in indirect forms even from the parents of the scholarship holders. So who paid whom? When the Dakshina Prize Committee used to give stipends, there was no complaint of any kind from any level of society. Then why now? Oh, well.

I passed my B.A. The figures in my B.A. mark-sheet were worthy of high praise. I had got good marks without falling behind in any way. Not only did I have respect for my teachers' fairness, but it made me happy too. But in human life, no joy is unmixed. It can't be attained fully without some little blemish. So now, the story of my M.A.

In the second year of our M.A. we went to the postgraduate department in the university. Very well-known scholars taught us there. The head of the department was a scholar of all-India repute. He didn't like my learning Sanskrit, and would make it clear that he didn't. And he took a malicious delight in doing so. The sharp claws of his taunts left my mind wounded and bleeding. In a way, I had developed a terror of this great pandit. His manner of speaking was honeyed and reasonable, but filled with venom. I would unconsciously compare him with Gokhale Guruji. I couldn't understand why this great man with a doctorate, so renowned all over India, this man in his modern dress, who did not wear the traditional cap, who could so eloquently delineate the philosophy of the Universal Being, and with such ease explain difficult concepts in simple terms, could not practise in real life the philosophy in the books he taught. This man had been exposed to modernity; Gokhale Guruji was orthodox. Yet one had been shrivelled by tradition, the other enriched by it, like a tree weighed down with fruit. Days go by; you survive calamities; but the memory of them sets up its permanent abode in you. In the inmost recesses of your inner being. I survived even through such a difficult ordeal. I got my M.A. with distinction.

A congratulatory bouquet of colourful, fragrant flowers came from Professor (Dr) Kolte, the former vice-chancellor of Nagpur University. I stared at it unblinkingly. In those flowers, I could see Dr Kolte's heart blossoming, petal by petal, with pride. And smell the sweet fragrance of unalloyed joy, thrilling my senses and arousing my self-confidence.

And now I would be a lecturer in Sanskrit! My dreams were tinted with turquoise and edged in gold. The images I nursed about myself were taking strange shapes in my mind. A high-paid job would come to me on a platter from the government. For I must have been the first woman from a scheduled caste to pass with distinction in Sanskrit. Every nook and cranny of my mind was filled with such hopes and expectations. But those ideas were shattered. My illusions proved as worthless as chaff. I became despondent about the efficiency of the government. I started attending interviews in private colleges. And that was a complete farce. Some said, "But how will you stay on with us, when you've passed so well?" (In other words, they must have wanted to say, "How will you work for less pay?") In other places, the moment I had been interviewed and stepped out of the room, there would be a burst of derisive laughter. I would hear words like sharp needles: "So now even these people are to teach Sanskrit! Government brahmins, aren't they?" And the ones who said this weren't even brahmins, but so-called reformers from the lower castes, who considered themselves anti-brahmin, and talked of the heritage of Jotiba Phule, and flogged the mass of the lower castes for their narrow caste-consciousness. And yet they found it distasteful that a girl from the mahar caste, which was one of the lower castes, should teach Sanskrit. When people like these, wearing hypocritical masks, are in responsible positions in society, it does not take even a minute for that society to fall.

Two years after my M.A., I was still unemployed. There must be many whose position is the same as mine. In my frustration I took a bold step to get out of the trap. I presented my case in writing to the Honourable Shri Jagjivan Ram, the noted minister in the Central Cabinet. I condemned the flimsy pretence of the state government and the administration that flouted the Constitution. My words had all the power of a sharp sword. For they were a cry from the heart of a person being crushed to death under the wheels of circumstance like the screeching of the eagle Jatayu in his last struggles.

The Honourable Minister Jagjivan Ram placed the letter before Pandit Nehru, who was astonished by it, and sent me an award of Rs 250, telling me to meet the chief minister of Maharashtra. Accordingly the chief minister of that time, Yashwantrao Chavan, sent me a telegram asking me to meet him. Within a day or two, one wire after another had electrified me into wondering who I'd suddenly become. Getting past the ranks of spearmen and macebearers at the government office was quite an ordeal. But finally I got to see the 'saheb'. Now, I thought, I would get a job at once—as a clerk in the government office, at least. A naive expectation. The chief minister made me fulsome promises in his own style. "We'll definitely make efforts for you—but you won't get a job in minutes; it'll take us some time. We'll have to give thought to it; have to hunt out something."

And with this assurance came a fine speech that qualified as an example of literature. "A student of Sanskrit is intoxicated with idealism. It is a deeply felt personal desire. You shouldn't run after a job. Involve yourself in research. Pursue your studies." Now the controls of endurance that restrained me started to break rapidly, and the words that had been bound within me broke out. "Saheb, if you can't give me a job, tell me so, clearly. I don't want promises. Promises keep false hopes alive. Research is the fruit of mental peace. How do you expect me to have mental peace, when I am starving? And I'm tired of speeches." I was fed up with life. Otherwise in AD 1960 it would have been impossible for a wretch like me even to stand before a dignitary like this, with all the power of *kartumakartumanyathakartum*, 'to do, omit to do, or do in another way', let alone speak out to him.

Waiting for a job, I passed the first year of an M.A. in English Literature. It was just an excuse to keep myself occupied. That year I got married—an intercaste marriage. That is a story by itself—a different glimpse of the nature of Indian society. Let that be the subject of another story. The surprising thing is that two months after my marriage, I got an assistant lecturership in a government college. Deputy Director Sahastrabuddhe, who was on the interview board, was amazed. "How did this girl remain unemployed for two years?" Dr Kolte's good will remained a constant support here, too. Today, I am a professor in the famous college where I studied, whose very walls are imbued with the respect I felt for that institution. But one thought still pricks me: the credit for Kumud Somkuwar's job is not hers, but that of the name Kumud Pawde. I hear that a woman's surname changes to match her husband's—and so does her caste. That's why I say that the credit of being a professor of Sanskrit is that of the presumed higher caste status of Mrs Kumud Pawde. The caste of her maiden status remains deprived.

Translated from Marathi by Priya Adarkar

OMPRAKASH VALMIKI

Born into the chuhra caste, one of the lowest of the untouchable communities in Uttar Pradesh, Omprakash Valmiki (1950–) has emerged as a prominent figure in Hindi literature. His autobiography, Joothan (1997) received much critical acclaim. In addition to this, he has published three collections of poetry and two collections of short stories. Valmiki has also written Dalit Sahitya ka Saundaryshaastra *(The Aesthetics of Dalit Literature, 2001), and a history of the Valmiki community,* Safai Devata *(The God of Hygiene, 2009).*

JOOTHAN

Our house was adjacent to Chandrabhan Taga's gher or cowshed. Next to it lived the families of Muslim weavers. Right in front of Chandrabhan Taga's gher was a little johri, a pond, which had created a sort of partition between the chuhras' dwellings and the village. The name of the johri was Dabbowali. It is hard to say how it got the name of Dabbowali. Perhaps because its shape was that of a big pit. On one side of the pit were the high walls of the brick homes of the tagas. At a right angle to these were the clay walls of the two or three homes of the jhinwars. After these there were more homes of the tagas.

On the edges of the pond were the homes of the chuhras. All the women of the village, young girls, older women, even the newly married brides, would sit in the open space behind these homes at the edges of the pond to take a shit. Not just under the cover of darkness but even in daylight. The purdah-observing tyagi women, their faces covered with their saris, shawls around their shoulders, found relief in this open-air latrine. They sat on Dabbowali's shores without worrying about decency, exposing their private parts. All the quarrels of the village would be discussed in the shape of a Round Table Conference at this same spot. There was muck strewn everywhere. The stench was so overpowering that one would choke within a minute. The pigs wandering in narrow lanes, naked children, dogs, daily fights, this was the environment of my childhood. If the people who call the caste system an ideal social arrangement had to live in this environment for a day or two, they would change their mind.

Our family lived in this chuhra basti. Five brothers, one sister, two chachas, one tau and his family. Chachas and tau lived separately. Everyone in the family did some or other work. Even then we didn't manage to get two decent meals a day. We did all sorts of work for the tagas, including cleaning, agricultural work and general labour. We would often have to work without pay. Nobody dared to refuse this unpaid work for which we got neither money nor grain. Instead, we got sworn at and abused. They did not call us by our names. If a person were older, then he would be called "Oe chuhre". If the person were younger or of the same age, then "Abey chuhre" was used.

Untouchability was so rampant that while it was considered all right to touch dogs and cats or cows and buffaloes, if one happened to touch a chuhra, one got contaminated or polluted. The chuhras were not seen as human. They were simply things for use. Their utility lasted until the work was done. Use them and then throw them away.

A Christian used to visit our neighbourhood. His name was Sewak Ram Masihi. He would sit with the children of the chuhras around him. He used to teach them reading and writing. The government schools did not allow these children to enrol. My family sent only me to Sewak Ram Masihi. My brothers were all working. There was no question of sending our sister to school. I learnt my alphabet in Master Sewak Ram Masihi's open-air school, a school without mats or rooms. One day, Sewak Ram Masihi and my father had an argument. My father took me to the Basic Primary School. There my father begged Master Har Phool Singh; "Masterji, I will be forever in your debt if you teach this child of mine a letter or two."

Master Har Phool Singh asked us to come the next day. My father went. He kept going for several days. Finally, one day I was admitted to school. The country had become independent eight years ago. Gandhiji's uplifting of the untouchables was resounding everywhere. Although the doors of the government schools had begun to open for untouchables, the mentality of the ordinary people had not changed much. I had to sit away from the others in the class, that too on the floor. The mat ran out before reaching the spot I sat on. Sometimes I would have to sit way behind everybody, right near the door. And the letters on the board from there seemed faded.

The children of the tyagis would tease me by calling me "chuhre ka". Sometimes they would beat me without any reason. This was an absurd tormented life that made me introverted and irritable. If I got thirsty in school, then I had to stand near the hand-pump. The boys would beat me in any case, but the teachers also punished me. All sorts of stratagems were tried so that I would run away from the school and take up the kind of work for which I was born. According to these perpetrators, my attempts to get schooling were unwarranted.

Ram Singh and Sukkhan Singh were also in my class. Ram Singh was a chamar and Sukkhan Singh was a jhinwar. Ram Singh's father and mother worked as agricultural labourers. Sukkhan Singh's father was a peon in Inter College. The three of us studied together, grew up together, experienced the sweet and sour moments of childhood together. All three of us were very good in our studies but our lower caste background dogged us at every step.

Barla village also had some Muslim tyagis who were called tagas as well. The behaviour of these Muslim tagas was just like that of the Hindu tagas. If we ever went out wearing neat and clean clothes, we had to hear their taunts that pierced deep inside like poisoned arrows. If we went to the school in neat and clean clothes, then our class fellows said, "Abey, chuhre ka, he has come dressed in new clothes." If one went wearing old and shabby clothes, then they said, "Abey, chuhre ke, get away from me, you stink."

This was our no-win situation. We were humiliated whichever way we dressed.

I reached fourth class. Headmaster Bishambar Singh had been replaced by Kaliram. Along with him had come another new teacher.

After the arrival of these two, the three of us fell on terrible times. We would be thrashed at the slightest excuse. Ram Singh would escape once in a while, but Sukkhan Singh and I got beaten almost daily. I was very weak and skinny those days.

Sukkhan Singh had developed a boil on his belly, just below his ribs. While in class, he used to keep his shirt folded up so as to keep the boil uncovered. This way the shirt could be kept clear of the puss on the one hand, and on the other, the boil protected from the blows of the teacher. One day while thrashing Sukkhan Singh, the-teacher's fist hit the boil. Sukkhan screamed with pain. The boil had burst. Seeing him flailing with pain, I too began to cry. While we cried, the teacher was showering abuse on us non-stop. If I repeated his abusive words here, they would smear the nobility of Hindi. I say that because many big-named Hindi writers had wrinkled their noses and eyebrows when I had a character in my short story *Bail ki Khal* (The Ox Hide) swear. Coincidentally, the character who swore was a brahmin, that is, the knower of Brahma, of God. Was it possible? Would a brahmin swear…?

The ideal image of the teachers that I saw in my childhood has remained indelibly imprinted on my memory. Whenever someone starts talking about a great guru, I remember all those teachers who used to swear about mothers and sisters. They used to fondle good-looking boys and invite them to their homes and sexually abuse them.

One day the Headmaster Kaliram called me to his room and asked: "Abey, what is your name?"

"Omprakash," I answered slowly and fearfully. Children used to feel scared just encountering the headmaster. The entire school was terrified of him.

"Chuhre ka?" Headmaster threw his second question at me.

"Ji."

"All right… See that teak tree there? Go. Climb that tree. Break some twigs and make a broom. And sweep the whole school clean as a mirror. It is, after all, your family occupation. Go… get to it."

Obeying the headmaster's orders, I cleaned all the rooms and the verandas. Just as I was about to finish, he came to me and said, "After you have swept the rooms, go and sweep the playground."

The playground was way larger than my small physique could handle and in cleaning it my back began to ache. My face was covered with dust. Dust had gone inside my mouth. The other children in my class were studying and I was sweeping. The headmaster was sitting in his room and watching me. I was not even allowed to drink water. I swept the whole day. I had never done so much work, being the pampered one among my brothers.

The second day, as soon as I reached school, the headmaster again put me to sweeping the school. I swept the whole day. I was consoling myself that I will go back to the class from tomorrow.

The third day I went to class and sat down quietly. After a few minutes the headmaster's loud thundering was heard:

"Chuhre ke, motherfucker, where are you hiding ... your mother..."

I had begun to shake uncontrollably. A tyagi boy shouted, "Master Saheb, there he is, sitting in the corner."

The headmaster had pounced on my neck. The pressure of his fingers was increasing. As a wolf grabs a lamb by the neck, he dragged me out of the class and threw me on the ground. He screamed: "Go sweep the whole playground... Otherwise I will shove chillies up your arse and throw you out of the school."

Frightened, I picked up the three day-old broom. Just like me, it was shedding its dried up leaves. All that remained were the thin sticks. Tears were falling from my eyes. I started to sweep the compound while my tears fell. From the doors and windows of the schoolrooms, the eyes of the teachers and the boys saw this spectacle. Each pore of my body was submerged in an abyss of anguish.

Just then my father passed by the school. He stopped abruptly when he saw me sweeping the school compound. He called me, "Munshiji, what are you doing?" Munshiji was the pet name my father had given me. When I saw him, I burst out sobbing. He entered the school compound and came towards me. Seeing me crying, he asked, "Munshiji, why are you crying? Tell me, what has happened?"

I was hiccupping by now. In between my hiccups, I told the whole story to my father: that the teachers had been making me sweep for the last three days; that they did not let me enter the classroom at all.

Pitaji snatched the broom from my hand and threw it away. His eyes were blazing. Pitaji who was always taut as a bowstring in front of others was so angry that his dense moustache was fluttering. He began to scream, "Who is that teacher, that progeny of Dronacharya, who forces my son to sweep?"

Pitaji's voice had echoed through the whole school. All the teachers, along with the headmaster came out. Kaliram, the headmaster, threatened my father and called him names. But his threats had no effect on Pitaji. I have never forgotten the courage and the fortitude with which my father confronted the headmaster that day. Pitaji had all sorts of weaknesses, but the decisive turn that he gave my future that day has had a great impact on my personality.

The headmaster had roared, "Take him away from here... The chuhra wants him educated... Go, go... Otherwise I will have your bones broken."

Pitaji took my hand and started walking towards our home. As he walked away, he said, loudly enough for the headmaster to hear, "You are a teacher... So I am leaving now. But remember this much, Master... This chuhre ka will study right here... In this school. And not just him, but there will be more coming after him."

Pitaji had faith that the tyagis of the village would chastise master Kaliram for his behaviour. But what happened was the exact opposite. Whosoever's door we knocked, the answer was,

"What is the point of sending him to school?" "When has a crow become a swan?"

"You illiterate boorish people, what do you know? Knowledge is not gained like this."

"Hey, if he asked a chuhra's progeny to sweep, what is the big deal in that?"

"He only got him to sweep; did not ask for his thumb in *gurudakshina* like Dronacharya."

And so forth.

Pitaji came back, tired and dejected. He sat up all night without food or drink. God knows how deep an anguish Pitaji went through. As soon as the morning broke, he took me along and went to the house of the pradhan, Sagwa Singh Tyagi.

As soon as the pradhan saw Pitaji, he said, "Abey, Chotan?... what is the matter? You have come so early in the morning."

"Chowdhri Saheb, you say that the government has opened the doors of the schools for the children of chuhras and chamars. And that headmaster makes this child of mine to come out of class and sweep all day instead of teaching him. If he has to sweep the school all day, then tell me when is he going to study?"

Pitaji was supplicating the pradhan. He had tears in his eyes. I was standing near him and looking at him.

The pradhan called me near him and asked, "Which class are you in?"

"Ji, the fourth."

"You are in my Mahendra's class?"

"Ji."

Pradhanji said to Pitaji, "Don't worry. Send him to school tomorrow."

The next day I went to school with fear stalking my heart. I sat in class with trepidation. Every second I worried that the headmaster was coming... Now he comes... At the slightest sound my heart pounded. After a few days, things calmed down. But my heart trembled the moment I saw Headmaster Kaliram. It seemed as though it wasn't a teacher who was coming towards me but a snorting wild boar with his snout up in the air.

Translated from Hindi by Arun Prabha Mukherjee

DEVANOORA MAHADEVA

*Devanoora Mahadeva (1948–) is a major Kannada writer and public in-
tellectual. Dyavanooru, his first collection of short stories, brought a new
sensibility to modern Kannada literature. As a young student, Mahadeva
joined the Rashtriya Swayamsevak Sangh, attracted by their 'Hindus are
one' slogan. He soon grew disenchanted, turned to socialism, and worked
with Nanjundaswamy and George Fernandes in building the socialist movement. He is one of the founders of Dalit Sangharsha Samiti. Odalala (1984)
and* Kusumabale *(1989) cemented his position as a major Kannada writer.
He is a recipient of the Sahitya Akademi Award (1990) and the Padmashri
(2011). "Dambaru Bandudu" (Tar Comes) is Mahadeva's favourite story.*

TAR COMES

An Overview of the Village

The dirt track that's just good enough for a bullock cart to amble
along starts like an alley from the village and winds for three miles
before joining the main road on which the buses ply. Back from the
main road, the route dips down to the village and, hedged in on both
sides by cacti, meanders around the banyan grove in which the spirits
reside, forks into three and then runs into the village. On either side
of the forked alleys are houses that stand so close together that, at
first sight, they seem to choke each other.

It is not a village that's known for anything. If one counts, there
would at most be some eighty households. There's not even a little
hotel there, like everywhere else. You can judge the place from that.
And then there are some four young men who have studied up to
high school, either at neighbouring Nanjangud or Mysore. Lakuma,
Rajappa, Madu and Shambu are their names.

The relation between the above names and the story to be told is
as follows: the village patel doesn't exactly like these characters. After

all, who could suffer these twits, born before one's own eyes, strutting around with their heads held high? It's always the same story, right since our fathers' times. These boys, heedless of upper caste or lower caste, run around with that holeya, Lakuma, as if they were born of the same womb. They had been warned through their fathers. You think they'd listen to their fathers? Everyone is waiting for those boys to be caught harassing some girl. That will be an opportunity to drag them to the village hall, strip them down to their underpants, tie them to a pole and flog them. There is the hope that the boys will certainly oblige.

A Road is Ordered

It was during such times that the order sanctioning a road for the village came from above. The patel's ample body puffed up even more. The news spread through the village like wildfire. It may be recalled in this connection that, some seven or eight years ago, when the minister had visited the village, the patel had personally garlanded him and handed him a lemon, and had said that a village worth its name should at least have a road, and had pleaded with the honourable minister to be magnanimous and sanction one. It was evening by the time the patel returned from Nanjangud that day. He brought the news that he himself was to be the road contractor and that, from then on, for months together, no one needed to look around for work, and also that, with the excess government money, the village temple was to be renovated. Every house in the village was agog with all this news.

In Front of the Village

It's been many days now since all this has happened. Now the village is a regular battlefield. The banyan trees that once stood spread against the sky, as high as the eye could see, have all been razed to the ground. To those who remember a village that was hidden behind a dense mat of banyan trees, this must look like a desert. There's not even a trace left to show that the trees were once there. Where they once stood, there are now machines running around. At the sight of these machines, with stone wheels that reach man-high, moving around belching smoke, let alone the village children, even the men and women forget themselves and watch fascinated. The clamour that rises from there spreads across the village and goes beyond. To anyone seeing the village from a distance, it will look like the site of some huge upheaval. But if you come closer, the people and the village are still what they were. If you talk to them, you will know them to be the same people. But they have changed beyond recognition—the black tar that is spread on the ground is also smeared all over them. The way they look! The way they move!

On one side, ten or fifteen young women sit with their saris tied around their heads and crush the gravel. One among them raises her thin voice and sings, "Come, come soon, Chenna Basavayya." Others prod her on, joining her in a chorus, which is heard even by those working at a distance. With the workers engrossed in their work, the whole place, for as far as a furlong, has a festive air about it. Measuring and digging, digging and levelling, levelling and sprinkling water, sprinkling water and bringing the blend of gravel and tar in a barrow and filling it in, filling it in and spreading it—all this on the other side. A machine that goes backwards and forwards. A *dhug-dhug* machine that levels. A fire-spitting machine that mixes the gravel, sand and tar together. For everything, a machine. How many of them! Each one a weird black-black form.

The patel is standing where the measuring is going on, with his hands folded in front of him. Suddenly he turns back. He takes a few steps forward. From the look on his face, even a child can see that the work is going well.

Hands and Mouths Tarred

Children everywhere are the same. The moment they leave the hamlet, they gather around the tar. When the elders scold them, they retreat; when the elders turn away, they are back again. All the children spend their evenings where the tar is melted. Even after night has fallen, they do not return to their houses. The elders have to come, spank them and take them back. But then, even the elders who come to take the children away can't help spending at least a few moments watching the miracle of road-making before they go back. And if, while going home, they hold the hands of the children, the tar from the children's hands will smear theirs. That's what happened when Rangappa came to bring his son back. Angered, he spanked his son, asking: "Is this what your master taught you in school?" The boy opened his mouth wide and started to cry. When Rangappa, losing patience, hit him on the mouth, the child cried even louder and put his hands into his mouth. The tar on his hands stuck to his mouth. The mouth was sealed and the crying stopped. Many such things happened every evening.

And then, it has become a habit with the women to bring home a ball of tar when returning from work. Apparently, some woman tried to plug a leak in a pot with the tar, and it worked like magic. Since then, in whichever corner of the village there is a leaking pot, the tar finds its way there. It has also become a practice to borrow tar from the households that maintain a ready stock of it.

A Letter to the Editor
The driver, who ran the big machine, commuted every day, back and forth from Nanjangud. One day, word spread that the paper he brought along with him carried news of the village. Everyone, instead of getting down to work, crowded around the driver. The patel was fuming. The news the paper carried about the village, read like this:

> Sir,
>
> This is with reference to the road that the Government in its magnanimity has sanctioned to our village and the construction that is presently going on. We have learnt that the road contractor, who is also the village patel, plans to utilize Government funds for the renovation of the temple. This is misuse of public funds. It is our prayer to the concerned authorities that they should ensure that no such thing takes place.

Aggrieved
One cannot say with certainty whether or not the roadwork continued that day. Shall we say it went on like it didn't? What had started off as one thing had begun to turn into something entirely different. The fear about what might be the outcome of all this spread through the streets of the village. As evening approached, the plot grew thicker and thicker. The patel had the drummer announce that every

household should send one person to the chavadi (village square) for a meeting. Night had just begun to fall and darkness enveloped the village. Outside, it was so dark that people couldn't see each other's faces. The dim light from within the houses fell out of the windows and was lost in the darkness.

The Chavadi

In the chavadi, the lantern spewed out abundant smoke and some light. Already a few men had spread themselves out as if they had nothing to do with what was going on. People started dropping in one by one. As the crowd grew, so did the bustle.

In a moment, the din that rose from there began to drown the village. The patel was seated in the centre. The light from the lantern fell straight on his face. You could see it sweating lightly and his forehead rhythmically wrinkle, unwrinkle and wrinkle again. You could see who was sitting in which far corner as their faces lit up when they struck a match to light a beedi. There was such a mob of people there.

Man 1: "Why don't you start?"

Man 2: "Everyone knows it. What is there to start, except the dressing down?"

Rajappa: "What does that mean, brother?"

Man 3: "You are the ones who know about meanings and things like that. Have we gone to school, like you?"

The shanbog: "Be quiet for a while. Patel, why don't you speak?"

The patel: "What is there to say?"

The shanbog: "Everyone knows that you are the ones who wrote the letter to disgrace the village. Are you people inclined to accept that?"

(*The shanbog looks at Lakuma, Rajappa, Shambu and Madu. They nod their heads as if to say yes. An uproar that pounds the chests of those standing outside looms from within.*)

The patel: "What wrong did you people see in that?"

(*The patel's words are heard like a crack. Not one opens his mouth.*)

Rajappa: "If you put the money that's meant for something into something else, what else did you expect?"

(The clamour rises again. The shanbog waves his hand. The noise dies out gradually.)

The patel: "Did I swallow the money for my children's sake? Or did I do it for the sake of the village and for God's work?"

Madu: "You might do it for anything, sir. You didn't use it for what it was meant for."

(The clamour rises again. This time louder than before. The shanbog, louder than the rest as usual. This time one or two men stand up.)

Man 1: "Don't you fellows have anything like gods, elders and things like that?"

Man 2: "If they did, would they get into this business?"

Man 3: "Enough, keep quiet. Why does everyone have to say something?"

Man 4: "Flog them. That'll set them right. They will talk straight."

Rajappa, Shambu and Shambu's father: "Who's that man? Come beat us then. We'll take care of that too. Your writ runs only till the tip of your nose."

The patel *(raising his voice)*: "Yes, sure. What you did was the right thing to do, I say."

Shambu: "And you think what you did is right. What's the point of this discussion?"

The patel: "What did you say? You have the audacity to talk back to me like that! Have I become so decrepit as to just stand here and take it from you?"

So saying, the patel clenched his fist and stood up like a shot. His head hit the lantern and broke the glass; the pieces fell tinkling to the ground. The lantern flickered until it finally died out, plunging the whole place into darkness. Pandemonium ensued. Everyone struggled to get out of the chavadi as soon as possible. It went on like this for a while, then everything was quiet. The houses in the village shut their doors.

News from Hosur

The village slept, dreaming perhaps of what had happened the previous night. As if to spoil the dream, a man from the neighbouring Hosur passed by in the early hours of the day. The words he left behind began to creep along the alleys of the village:

> Sir, I am from Hosur. In our village, there was a dirty woman. It was her practice to seduce all the teenaged boys of the village. How long could one try to talk her out of it? She paid no heed. They tried scolding her, but she ignored them. Finally they did what had to be done. They called the village council meeting and dragged her there. Even there she was her usual arrogant self. Furious, they didn't leave it at that. They stripped her and flogged her with a tamarind branch, and made her rue the day she was born.
>
> Yet, she wouldn't let it go at that. She carried the same face straight to the police station. They say she told the police everything in detail: they did this to me, they did that to me. The police van arrived and rounded up all the landlords. Nobody knows what happened after that.

The news from Hosur blended with what was already brewing in the village, and the ferment rose higher and higher. They talked of what had happened.

The patel: "Hmm."

The shanbog: "Ha."

The Foursome: "Oh my god! They were lording it over. Now they've been shown their place."

Man 1: "*Ayyo*, Shiva!"

Tar in the Pit, in the Pitch of the Night

But things didn't stop there. Remember the tar drums that had been heated and kept in front of the village? The next morning, they were not to be seen. If you followed their trail, it led you outside the village. They had been arranged around a pit where, with their mouths wide open, they were spewing out tar in thick lumps. As the sun rose higher and higher, the tar continued pouring out into the pit, stretching gently out of the mouths of the drums. Those who had gathered round to see, kept watching. Those who hadn't seen it yet, came to see it in flocks. After they had watched and watched, and the blackness of it had filled their eyes, they would slowly move away. Nobody had a word to say.

Even the patel didn't have a word to say. One man said to the patel: "You should have just said yes, we would have beaten the daylights out of them last night." Even at that, the patel only clenched his teeth. Didn't say a word. He went to the police station straight from there. It was evening when he came back. It became known that, the next day, early in the morning, the police would come to carry out the investigations, and that no one could now say what turn it would all take.

The One Who Went to the Hamlet Hasn't Returned

As one thing led to another and the plot grew darker and darker, and as the village waited for night to fall, there was yet another thing that would come to pass. Although it was dusk and every house had closed its door, and there was not a soul stirring in the streets, Rangappa's child still hadn't come back home. Apparently he had headed towards the hamlet after lunch. They asked the schoolmaster, who said he had seen the boy walk homewards. He was the kind of dumb child that headed straight to wherever he was going. With a lantern in hand, they knocked at every house in the village. They asked his playmates. No one had seen him. Not a single street, not a single alley was left unsearched. How long could this continue? His mother's cry was the only sound in the silent village and she wailed through the night.

Investigations

At dawn, the police van came bumping along with difficulty and stopped in front of the village. The inspector sent off a man who was standing around to bring the patel along. The patel hurried out to the spot. Everyone gathered around the pit outside the village to look, and froze the moment they saw. The tar in the pit had trapped Rangappa's child, and the tar drum had both his hands. His hands, his body and face were all covered with tar. And if you took a closer look, in that child's body, there was life still throbbing.

Translated from Kannada by Manu Shetty and A.K. Ramanujan

H. GOVINDAIAH

H. Govindaiah (1954–) inspired by the revolutionary dalit struggles of his time found solace in poetry, despite being a student of economics. He was actively associated with Dalit Sangharsha Samiti (DSS) and publisher of Panchama, *a fortnightly magazine of DSS for 10 years until 1985. Govindaiah's "A Aa Mattu" (A Aa And) has been used in various textbooks. He has worked as a lecturer at Mysore University and the Karnataka Open University and was Deputy Registrar of the latter for two years.*

A LETTER TO FATHER

Father,
The application that I had submitted then
Has earned me a job today.
Don't keep looking for me anymore.
Don't ask the gowda to write
a 'missing' ad for the paper.
Tell Mother also not to cry. Tell her
I will be back home anytime now.

The job is in our village itself—
or in a surrounding one
(it's not temporary, you see).
Until then the work here
is to build a dam,
generate electricity.
We plan to supply it to our village as well.
Salary will be paid in a lump sum,
after the dam is built.

When Mother was ill,
for the loan he gave—glaring derisively at me—
if the gowda insists that it be repaid
with bonded labour,
tell younger brother to ready himself
to go and drudge.
I too will come.
Tell the gowda ... Father,
tell him without fail,
I will come and clear it.

Translated from Kannada by Ankur Betageri

REKHARAJ

Born into a family of prominent dalit intellectuals, Rekharaj (1978–) struggles with the representation of the dalit woman in feminist scholarship and in dalit discourses. She has contributed essays and criticism to mainstream journals like Madhyamam, Bhashaposhini *and* Mathrubhumi *as well as little magazines like* Sameeksha. *The article here was written in the context of the widespread protests that followed the suicide of a young dalit engineering student, Rajani S. Anand, in July 2004.*

RAJANI'S SUICIDE

The suicide of Rajani, a student of a private engineering college in Adoor, alarms us all in many ways. Particularly disturbing are the views and reactions expressed by the administration following the event. A social analysis of Rajani's tragic life that goes beyond the turmoil and the protests that ensued after the suicide is necessary.

There has been much commotion within most students' organizations and particularly in those led by the Left after the Rajani incident. Most of these have addressed the issue through a variety of clichés like the problem of the government's policy on higher education, or the attitude of banks towards providing loans for students from an underprivileged background. My intention is not to suggest that these problems are not serious, but that there are far more fundamental and deeper issues that might actually be the cause of these problems.

Most dalit students cannot avail of facilities like bank loans as parental property is the guarantee against which banks lend money to students. When this policy of the banks is interpreted as anti-working class, matters acquire a certain simplistic certitude. Yet, clearly, treating this merely as a problem of either fundamental rights or of class is insufficient. Unless the reality that the ownership of property in Kerala is *caste* based is firmly established, it will be impossible to reveal the connection between the fundamental problems detailed above.

It is possible to treat Rajani's death as a dalit issue because it highlights the acute challenges facing the dalit community at the moment. It is not necessary to spell out that the lives of Rajani's dalit student contemporaries are extremely complex. The government is in the process of privatizing higher education and almost completely removing it from the public sphere. Dalit students are forced to study outdated courses in government institutions at a time when private, self-financing colleges are offering courses geared towards better possibilities, knowledge and job opportunities. With such an education, they are faced with the perils of unemployment and are even forced to enter construction work or other manual labour. Most dalit girls become sales girls with lowly wages. The incompetent contemporary education system, instead of distilling and enhancing talents, succeeds in cleverly pushing out dalit students from technological institutions. They are forced to remain shackled within oppressive institutions and are unable to choose the new knowledge domains like IT and management. Education is unable to open up the way towards modernization or employment—as we imagine it should. The dalit community is seeking keenly a generation that is able to face its challenges in an intelligent, practical and creative manner.

The above-mentioned dalit experiences were the ones that Rajani attempted to challenge, knowingly or unknowingly. She courageously entered and bolstered her self-confidence in a realm that would have been unavailable or unwelcoming to her in the natural course of things. By entering the computer science (degree) course through the merit list, she was dispelling the charge of 'unmeritorious' often levelled against dalit students. Rajani committed suicide because of her inability to continue in the professional course given the inadequacy of the government stipend and the refusal by the banks to provide a loan.

In this context, there is absolutely no reason for Rajani's sexual life becoming a topic of discussion. However, the equation that a dalit woman is equal to a bad woman/immoral woman persists on the strength of societal prejudice. At the same time, the dalit movement's attempts to reform the family and the women's movements' idealization of subaltern sexuality share the same societal prejudice. This suicide makes us aware that an approach based on closer scrutiny and greater alertness is an immediate necessity.

Translated from Malayalam by G. Arunima

SUKIRTHARANI

Born in Lalapet, Vellore district of Tamil Nadu, Sukirtharani (1973–) is now considered an important Tamil poet. At school, she used to be given two of her textbooks free and had to borrow the rest, but despite that she always topped the class. A rebel from childhood, she explains that she hated the word "Don't" which was always more frequently addressed to her than to her brothers. With her M.A., B.Ed. and M.Phil., she teaches Tamil in a government school. Her writing is considered radical, polished and intellectual. She has published five volumes of poetry.

UNTITLED POEM

With handfuls of poems
I come to you;
You wait for me
with countless kisses.
In a kiss, several poems—
In a poem, several kisses
slip away from us.

PARIAH GOD

You say
the heat that sears your side
is a pariah sun.
You say
the beak that steals
the worm-ridden grain spread out to sun
is a pariah crow.
You say

the mouth that snatches
food along with your wrist
is a pariah dog.
When the land is tilled
and sweat is sown,
you say
it is pariah labour.
If this is how everything is named,
what is the name of that pariah god
who walks the earth blood-thirsty?

Translated from Tamil by Meena Kandasamy

B. KRISHNAPPA

The founder-president of the Dalit Sangharsha Samiti, B. Krishnappa (1938–97) was a pioneer of the dalit literary movement and radical dalit politics in Karnataka. He studied Kannada, being unable to afford to study medicine as his family desired, and taught at the Sir M. Vishweshwaraiah College in Bhadravathi for thirty years—retiring as principal. He made his mark as a critic of Kannada literature. A social revolutionary, both in his personal and private life—he married Indira, a brahmin student in his college—Krishnappa's presence is felt in most of the landmark dalit struggles in the state, especially those aimed at getting land for dalits and fighting for dalit women's self-respect.

DALIT LITERATURE

Can literary texts about dalits be considered dalit literature? Or is dalit literature necessarily written by dalits? This is the question before us today.

If we are to consider dalit literature as literature about dalits, then Pampa's *Karna*, Harihara's *Madara Chennaiah*, Basavanna's vachanas, Raghavanka's *Holatiyaru Mattu Veerabahu* (Holeya Women and Veerabahu), and in modern literature, Shivarama Karanth's *Chomana Dudi* (Choma's Drum), U.R. Ananthamurthy's *Bharathipura*, Gorur Ramaswamy Iyengar's *Hemavathi*, Kuvempu's *Malegalalli Madumagalu* (The Bride of the Hills) and P. Lankesh's *Sankramana* (Transition) would have to be deemed dalit literature. But just because Pampa has written about a dalit, can he be called a dalit writer? Similarly, how can Harihara, Raghavanka, Basavanna, Karanth, Ananthamurthy, Gorur and Kuvempu be called dalit writers?

What is more, Pampa, Harihara, Karanth and Kuvempu would not aspire to be known as dalit writers. In a 1978 special issue of *Prajavani*, responding to a question about whether literary movements are created only by writers, Karanth says he cannot measure literature through the lens of caste. When caste is such a pulsating reality, one can't but call his response casual. When he is not ready to consider himself a dalit, how can one call his writings dalit literature? It is in this regard that the dalit writers of Maharashtra have rejected the idea that Keshavsut's poem about a mahar boy, S.M. Mate's stories about mahars, and more recently Jaywant Dalvi's *Chakra* are dalit literature.

Conversely, if a writer is a dalit by birth, is his work necessarily dalit literature? Only recently, post-independence, did dalits win the right to literacy. D.R. Nagaraj cites the vachanas of Madara Chennaiah, composed in the context of the twelfth-century vachana movement, as a rare early exception. However, the dalits' feeling of inferiority and a reluctance to admit their identity even post independence persists to this today. In 1974, when the first Dalit Sahitya Sammelana was held in Bhadravathi, some gentlemen I wrote to assuming they were dalits did not even respond to my letters. Sri Channanna Walikar, who is now vociferously talking about dalit literature, never came to the Sammelana. He was to preside over the poets' session. In his absence, K.N. Shivatheerthan presided over it. Sri G. Venkatayya, who was to inaugurate our Sammelana, is a very good dalit writer. But can the writings of Banandoor Kempayya and Paramashiva Nadubetta, who had also attended the Sammelana, and Chandrashekar Kambar, whose dalit origins were only recently blown up by the Sahitya Parishat, be called dalit literature? If you ask me, I would say "no". I say this because, in their writings, I do not see a commitment to dalit literature. They may be born dalits, but they lack commitment to their identity. Surely then, they cannot aspire to be dalit writers; neither will they make a valuable contribution to the body of dalit literature. Here, I should talk about the exclusion of some African poets from what is thought of as African literature.

Camara Laye is a well-regarded African poet. His *Dark Child* and *Dream of Africa* are well-known writings. In his *Dream of Africa*, he asks black people to stop even their non-violent protests. Though Laye is committed to his blackness, African nationalists term him a colonialist potboiler writer because nowhere in his writings does he protest against British colonialism. So the nationalists are against his inclusion in black literature. In the same way, they are against the inclusion of Amos Tutuola, who refuses to remain committed to any position, because they believe that African literature demands certain commitments:

1. Recognizing the oppression of the blacks by the whites; rejecting the assumption that white or red is superior and black inferior, and the slavish attitude that racial prejudice has given rise to.

2. Protesting against colonial and capitalist tendencies.

3. Endorsing Leftist ideology, and

4. Exhibiting pride in the rich culture of Africa, the land of negritude and of black people.

In effect, a black writer anywhere in the world must protest against the system that discriminates against people on the basis of colour and subjects them to slavery. Colonial and imperialistic British forces, by occupying Africa, snatched away its freedom. Inevitably, every black writer aspiring to freedom should protest this act. Besides, in a situation where the people have been pushed to dire poverty and must gain economic equality through political philosophy, manifesto and support, a writer who tries to achieve this through his writings will be regarded highly by his people. His experiences as a victim of racial discrimination and imperialism would be a value addition to his corpus of his writings. Instead, if a black poet begins to think like a white person and supports colonialism, it signals his alienation from his African self, despite being born an African. The same is true of a dalit.

India's five-thousand-year history may be celebrated as glorious and magnificent, but concealed within its fringes are some terrible injustices. Its caste system, brahminical and hierocratic, enforced the exclusion of entire communities from the village. They were required to live outside the village limits. It deemed them unworthy of touch or sight. It ascribed to them the task of scavenging and of consuming dead cattle. The self-anointed brahmin, at the top of the caste system, exploited people in the name of the gods, the Vedas and the puranas. He proclaimed that only he had the right to learning. So, for the last five thousand years, unaware of their real self, the hard-working shudra and the dirt-cleaning dalits have lived in the dark, ignorant of learning, like animals. Whoever calls this history great must be treated with molten lead.

The dalit literature I mentioned earlier may be small in quantity, but is superior in quality. However, there are some who say, "They only scream '*Ikkrala, Vadirla*',[1] is that literature?"

Dalit literature has a different stand on creativity and literary excellence. It is inappropriate to look for refinement in a movement's revolutionary literature. That kind of art can only be found in a literature written in luxury. Refinement cannot be the mainstay of a literature that has revolution and change as its goals.

The purpose of literature that is part of a revolution and has the common people as its focus will have to be different. As dalit literature is addressed more to the labourer, the farm hand toiling in the fields, the unfortunate living in hell, suppressed by the caste system, it has to be unadorned and fresh.

When the purpose is to provoke people against injustice, there is no scope for old aesthetic pleasures or artistic creativity or, indeed, abstruse similes and metaphors. Dalit literature is not the literature of those whose stomachs are full.

Progressive literature is only one wave in dalit literature. By itself, it cannot be revolutionary literature. On the other hand, there is little difference between dalit literature and revolutionary literature. The purpose of dalit literature is to prepare people for revolution. This being the case, any literature that is communal, religious or pro-capitalist will automatically be anti-dalit. Not just that, literature that makes enough noise about the poor and the suppressed, but fails to recognize caste, religion and class as vehicles of exploitation, will also be anti-dalit. Writing is a challenging task for those who are actively immersed in revolution or protest. The extent to which they will take on this challenge will determine the quality of their work. The work of a writer who takes no part in such movements may acquire fame

---

[1] "Bash them, kick them." The reference is to the famous poem "Ondu Pada" (A Song) by Siddalingaiah, whose other poems are featured in this volume.

merely by the quantity of output, but quality-wise, it can only be regarded as boosa [cattle feed]. Some time ago, I had agreed to attend the Dharmasthala Sahitya Sammelana with the intention of putting forward these views. It was not yet clear then whether the Bandaya Sahitya Sammelana would be held separately. But when it became clear that holding a separate meeting had become inevitable, I was clear that I would attend the Bandaya meeting rather than a boosa revolutionaries' forum, like the Dharmasthala Sahitya Sammelana. I felt it was my duty to reject the latter's invitation. It is indeed unfortunate that, despite this, the president of the Dharmasthala Sahitya Sammelana wrote again, pressing me to participate in the event.

Literature produced by the satiated and the flabby, who consume antacids to digest their food, who live in multi-storeyed buildings and commute only by car and airplane, has no appeal for me. For such people, literature is an aesthetic luxury, written to kill time. Protest literature is not written for this Tata-Birla five percent who lead a lavish life.

Our engagement today is with the starving, the helpless, those who eat from the waste bins outside hotels, the homeless who live in railway stations, bus stands, those who steal food and clothing and die without a history. Aesthetics is not primary for us. When over 60 per cent of our population live below the poverty line, shedding their blood in fields and factories and rotting in ignorance, anyone who says that he writes for aesthetic pleasure, or for literary values, can only be called irresponsible.

That we have produced such irresponsible literature for the last fifty years is indeed surprising. Poetry, instead of being realistic (objective), became simply imaginative (subjective). With people writing in the subjective mode, having no fixed positions or commitments, the genre acquired a cynical quality. For some it became spiritual; it gnawed at others who were overwhelmed by a sense of being orphaned. To my knowledge, no Kannada writer has dwelt on the real problems of this country—the caste system that made life in India gruesomely cruel, and kept one-fourth, no half, of the population outside the village limits, suppressed them and exploited them physically and culturally. Caste plays an important role even to this day. Be it elections or political office, caste is a living force, eating its way into human lives like termites.

Translated from Kannada by Maithreyi M.R.

MATHIVANNAN

Mathivannan (1971–) began writing poetry while still at school. He has been actively associated with the arundathiyar movement in Tamil Nadu. His poetry and essays reflect the contemporary concerns of the movement. Mathivannan has published two volumes of poetry, Nerindhu *(The Strangled One, 2000), and* Namakkidaiyilana Tholaivu *(The Distance between Us, 2005), and a book of essays. He works as a certified radiological assistant.*

SCAVENGER'S SON
IN THE COLLECTIVE THINKING OF TAMIL WRITERS

Most writing on dalits by non-dalits has come from progressive writers. These writers have not experienced dalit life. The perspective projected in their writings is a combination of their own caste-centred life and what they have observed and heard about the life of a dalit. Such works are based on information about dalits and provide an overhead view. A dalit reader finds this alienating. Thakazhi Sivasankara Pillai's *Scavenger's Son* is a good example of such writing.[1]

However, mainstream, classical writers such as Sundara Ramaswamy clearly approve of the novel. He has translated it from Malayalam to Tamil.

"My mind was filled with wonder and fondness when I read *Scavenger's Son*. How elegantly this writer has told this story and made it

---

[1] Thakazhi Sivasankara Pillai (1912–99) is an iconic Malayalam Leftist writer. He was a prolific writer and acclaimed as a realist. He depicted the lives of working-class people in Kerala, most famously that of scavengers (*Thotiyude Makan—Scavenger's Son*, 1947), fisherfolk (*Chemeen—*Shrimps, 1956) and coirworkers (*Kayar—*Rope, 1978). Here Mathivannan, an arundathiyar, takes on the nair author as well as his brahmin translator.

memorable. How did he manage to move with such ease into that dark, hidden world and bring out their feelings? When I realized that what Thakazhi has exposed is not just the feelings of the scavengers, but the flames lit in the recesses of their minds by time, I was filled with awe." This is the translator, Sundara Ramaswamy, writing in his introduction. He goes ecstatic.

However, a dalit reader finds the Tamil version, coming as it does fifty years after the original, disappointing and tedious. That this novel was written fifty years ago is not what triggers this reaction. When you compare the popularity enjoyed by the works of fiction of Daniel and Poomani, written only a little later than Thakazhi's novel, you realize the time is not a factor here. What is critical in generating such a response is the perspective of the writer. Though this work of Thakazhi is *about* the lives of scavengers, the pertinent question is from what angle does he look at their lives? We can get an idea of his point of view from the following lines:

"If you look carefully, you can observe in his eyes that he does not have the cowardice, the utter lack of self-esteem and a feeling of worthlessness of a scavenger." (p. 33)

Scavengers are cowards. They have no self-worth. If this is the idea that those who set out to document the lives of sanitary workers have, what kind of a story will emerge from them? You have a good example in *Scavenger's Son*.

Sudalaimuthu is the son of one of the scavengers brought from the Tirunelveli area to work in Alleppey municipality. Sudalaimuthu dreams that somehow his son should be made into a respectable man and not end up as a scavenger. Working towards this goal, he indulges in mean activities, going to the extent of betraying his colleagues. The municipal chairman cheats him of the money he had earned through illegal means and Sudalaimuthu dies uncared for in a cholera epidemic. In the end, his son too becomes a scavenger. Thakazhi makes this a maudlin narrative against the backdrop of the lives of scavengers. Without a regular income, without a place to live, they struggle on and die like flies in cholera and smallpox epidemics. Their life is a poignant tragedy.

Two important questions arise out of this novel. The novelist could not find an honest scavenger to depict in his story. He has chosen a selfish betrayer like Sudalaimuthu around whom to weave his story. Why? Why was not a character like Pichandi, principled, sensitive to class struggle and compassionate, made the central figure?

Similarly, why has not the writer chosen to set his story in a period of the awakening of scavengers instead of in an earlier oppressive period? For one who set out to write a progressive novel, would not the later period have been suitable?

There could be only one answer to these questions. It is the result of Thakazhi Sivasankara Pillai's hegemonic perspective. Thakazhi is convinced that scavengers are cowards, fools, are easily cheated and therefore get exploited. Moreover, they are in the grip of selfish men. He thinks: this is the reason for their degradation in this social system. So to some extent, they themselves are responsible. Yet, as a progressive writer, it is my (Thakazhi's) responsibility to be kind to them. The progressive formula seems to be adequate to write the story of scavengers. If you add a procession with red flags here and the slogan 'Long Live the Revolution' there, then it gets the label of a brilliant, progressive work. Who can question this?

If you ignore the rather pompous statement made by Sundara Ramaswamy in the introduction—"what Thakazhi has exposed is the fire lit by time in the recesses of scavengers' minds"—Thakazhi's archaic hegemonic attitude that is no different from a commonplace perspective may be perceived.

This collective mind that he represents, cannot conceive of scavengers without connecting them with the arse and the shit that comes through it. This is what Thakazhi has done throughout his work. Even when they talk among themselves, the scavengers discuss only latrines, the different types of them, those who shat there and what they had eaten. The scavenger finds even a newborn infant smelling of shit.

When a father fondles his child, what kind of thoughts would arise in his mind? According to Thakazhi, this is what a scavenger father would think:

"I wonder if this infant is also disgusted. Can it smell the stench? Ever after a bath, a scavenger stinks."

He is concerned that if he touches the child there might be some mishap. He wants the infant to grow up without ever touching a scavenger. In another context Thakazhi writes that even when he proceeds to feed the baby the thought of the hundreds of latrines he entered surfaces in his mind.

You see this atrocious attitude of Thakazhi pervading throughout the novel. Compared to this, the approach of Kesavapillai, a character in the novel, who ridicules the scavengers by saying, "Do not consider these fellows as human beings," would seem better.

If you observe which characters Thakazhi takes seriously, you get a better insight into his hegemonic attitude. Those who fight injustice and are focused on their goal, appear in the novel as phantoms without names. They are referred to as son of Sundaram, son of Pichandi and so on. The scavengers who are identified or considered important are those who are slavish. And they are known by their names: Isakimuthu, Yoseppu, Sudalaimuthu, Pazhani, Sundaram and Munusami. Is this because Thakazhi recognizes the slavish mentality of the scavengers as their distinctive character? Scavengers are identified by their degradation. And the sons of scavengers are identified by the degradation of their fathers.

This is the source of the stench that pervades the novel. What has been created by the hand that has kneaded the shit called casteism will, of course, stink.

Sundara Ramaswamy says in his introduction that he translated this novel when he was unknown in the literary world. But his is a poor translation. Even if he tries again he cannot produce a worse translation. This is a translation published fifty years after the novel was written. Perhaps there are marketing considerations in its publication. But no one seems to have checked the text before publishing it. There is no evidence to show that it has been edited.

"Those eyes seem to look at Sudalaimuthu. A bluish acid drips from the eyes of the corpse" (p. 28). When you read about acid from the eyes of the dead body, please do not get confused and imagine that this is a piece of magical realism. Liquid is referred to as acid by the translator (*dhravagam* instead of *dhiravam*).

Similarly, the way in which the scavengers from Tirunelveli speak is hilarious. Now they speak in brahminical Tamil; and now in the Kanyakumari district style. The result is altogether comical. [Mathivannan provides several examples of comical dialect mixing, which we have not been able to translate effectively.] One can cite such instances throughout the novel. Moreover, many Sanskrit words, such as *sisruchai* (nursing care), *thitasangalbam* (determination) and *hasyam* (humour) are strewn through the narrative. Quite annoying.

Translated from Tamil by Theodore Baskaran

ARAVIND MALAGATTI

An author, a critic and a poet, Aravind Malagatti (1956–) received the Karnataka Sahitya Academy Award for his autobiography, Government Brahmana *(1994). Malagatti, a consistent presence in the dalit movement, is now professor of Kannada at Mysore University. He has authored over ten volumes of poetry, a novel, and several plays in addition to numerous academic articles and books. He is a folklore scholar, a fact that shines through in the following excerpt from* Government Brahmana.

THE SHE-BUFFALO ON HEAT AND THE HE-BUFFALO AFTER HER

Isn't it said that the crow, the owl, the dog, the donkey, the sheep and the bison are rishi Vishwamitra's creations, while the pigeon, the horse, the cow and animals such as these are rishi Vasishta's creations? It seems the brahmin sage Vasishta could create pure, white, sweet voiced, sweet tempered, mild and beautiful animals and birds, and rishi Vishwamitra could create only those with the opposite qualities. Having been a king once, the non-brahmin rishi Vishwamitra could never rise to the status of brahmarishi—that is, a supreme rishi like Vasishta—despite his hard penance. Doesn't this myth indicate that it is natural for a nonbrahmin to be denied the status of brahmarishi? These myths are so deep-rooted that while you think you have uprooted them completely, they will spring up like weeds—such is their nature. Some also have this to say:

> Look, how many castes exist
> among animals, birds and plants.
> How can there not be caste among men? Think a little.
> Among cows, dogs, donkeys, tigers,
> cats, pigs, fox, rats,
> deer, monkeys, fish—how many castes are there?
> Likewise among men,

Whites, blacks, tribes, harijans,
Chinese, Japanese, Turks, Mongolians,
Aryans, Dravidians, brahmana, shudra...
Brahmana Bandaya

Yes. If one were to think carefully, there are a variety of birds and fish. No doubt, birds and fish of the same kind live together. Since tiny creatures like fish have several castes and they abide by them, if you say that a human being too should do so, why should he be called an intelligent animal? Is it wise to differentiate among human beings as superior and inferior? Surely, posing this argument, in the twentieth century, is nothing but sowing more seeds of venom in the guise of planting something new (within the framework of mythology).

The poem has some sense in it, theoretically and logically. But logic is not fully applied here. Look, a male horse mates with a female horse and produces offspring. Similarly a dog mates with a bitch to produce puppies. Can a horse mate with a bitch? No! So what is caste after all? It is a group of similar animals that can mate with their females and produce offspring. Therefore, there is no problem in saying that 'horse' is a caste, and human beings together are one caste. Blacks, whites, Chinese, Japanese, Mongolians, Turks, tribes, harijans, shudras, brahmins ... irrespective of the categories, men and women can have natural physical relations with each other and produce children. True, different castes cannot naturally mingle.

Indeed there is a close relationship between the human kind and the animal kind! Beliefs, practices, traditions and mythologies influence and inform this relationship. Just thinking about it makes me shudder and causes my hair to rise! I was probably a nine- or ten-year-old boy then. My aayi used to tell us that the only she-buffalo in our lane used to be in our house. It was the offspring of the she-buffalo that was sent as gift to my aayi by her parents. Aayi was thus proud of owning the only she-buffalo in the lane.

"I was born after my seven brothers.
My parents brought me up like a boy,
feeding me milk, curds, butter and ghee in abundance.
Therein lies the secret of my strength.

Your muthya was hardly strong.
Used to pant, to carry a pot of water from the village outskirts!
I used to carry water in a pot twice the size on my head,
and on the waist, a pot one and half times larger!
People who saw this would say,
'Ye, Yellavva, if one *does,* they should bear a girl like you.'"
To this, my aayi would add:
"For me to be like this, what varieties of food
I must have eaten in my house!
That's why my mother sent a she-buffalo with me—
so that I'd be happy in my in-laws' house too.
When I came here what was there in this house?
Everything was hanging like the bell around the buffalo's neck."
Given the slightest chance, my aayi would untie her sack of memories. The story of the she-buffalo—her dowry—would variably follow.

I do not know what had happened to the she-buffalo that day. She was mooing continuously since that morning as if her throat would tear. My avva took her for grazing in that condition. She came back grumbling,
"She ran everywhere, and made me run around too.
My feet are hurting from running behind her.
May the devil take her..."
She grumbled loud enough for my aayi to hear. Of course, she had not failed to notice that the buffalo was on heat.

There was no he-buffalo in our village to mate with our she-buffalo. But in two neighbouring villages, Kuntoji and Basarkod, there were two he-buffaloes. These buffaloes belonged to the village heads. There is no use raising he-buffaloes in the hot plains. They cannot be used for ploughing as they lack the capacity to withstand heat. So, common people never reared he-buffaloes. For the village gowda and desai, it was a matter of prestige to rear he-buffaloes. There is a proverb that goes "The chief's buffalo neither rode, nor let others ride." All that these he-buffaloes had to do was ride the she-buffaloes that were on heat. The he-buffalo was not only the king of all buffaloes in the village but also the emperor of the buffaloes in the neighbouring villages.

Usually, he-buffaloes born in the village were swallowed up by deities like Dyamavva, Durugavva and Murugavva. Or else they ended up at the steps of the slaughterhouse, singing their last songs. There were no chances of survival for these he-buffaloes. Therefore, the village gowda's and desai's he-buffaloes were in great demand.

Kuntoji is closer to our place than Basarkod. My aayi decided to take the buffalo to Kuntoji. But it was already dusk. It would be completely dark before one reached Kuntoji. They would not let the he-buffalo mate with our she-buffalo in the night. So Aayi decided to start at dawn. I, who had been listening to these discussions with curiosity, made up my mind to go to Kuntoji. So I started tailing Aayi wherever she went.

While my worry was that I would be left behind, my aayi had another. If the she-buffalo slept, she would come out of heat. So one had to watch her through the night to prevent her from falling asleep. I stepped in, on the pretext of helping aayi:

"Aayi, if you want to go somewhere, you can go now.

I'm willing to keep an eye on the she-buffalo."

Instructing me, "If she falls asleep, beat her and wake her up," my aayi went away. The buffalo would not stay awake despite my beatings. So, we (my brothers were also with me) would scream aloud before it could fall asleep.

"Aayi … eee … Aayi, come soon."

The buffalo, frightened by our commotion, could not rest even for a fraction of a second. Aayi watched and waited, leaning against the pole of the cowshed the whole night. I roamed around restlessly, and finally slept holding the end of Aayi's sari for fear that she would leave me behind and set off alone at dawn!

The journey started at dawn. Despite Aayi's objections, I remained stubborn and finally convinced her to take me along. Though the two villages were quite far, they were not new to us. The villages were quite famous for their fairs and Okuli. We never failed to attend the feast usually held during the fair with our aayi. I reminded her of all those instances and convinced her that I could walk to those villages. The road to Kuntoji had been laid with tar, but not the road to Basarkod. The road to Basarkod was wonderful. The regular traffic of bullock carts had made grooves of equal depth on the road that it looked like a railway track. And on that railway track was fine powder-like soil. Walking on it was like walking on snow. With every step came the sound *psk* and the buttery soft soil was squeezed up through the toes. Especially at dawn, it was immensely cool and pleasing.

It was annoying to walk on the tar road and not the nice Basarkod road. When I said, "Let us go to Basarkod," so that we could enjoy the walk, perhaps even Aayi felt the same.

"Yes, it's better to go there perhaps!

But what to do...

Who knows what that rascal might do?"

Muttering, she chose the road to Kuntoji. When we reached the tar road after passing our village, we saw a bullock cart going to Kuntoji. She pleaded,

"Appa! Ey appa!

Small boy, can't walk.

Comes behind me, though I say no. He doesn't listen to me.

Give him a lift please ... appa..."

Whenever I went somewhere with Avva or Aayi, such pleas were common. As soon as they began imploring, I would sport an expression of being tired and worn out. While some, moved by the request, let us ride in their carts, others who knew that we were untouchables drove away quickly. But that did not happen in this case. As soon as my aayi asked the fellow, he let us board his cart. Chatting throughout the journey, we reached Kuntoji.

"May you have all the luck, appa.

Like he has blessed me, may god

bless you also with good grandchildren!"

Blessing him in a brahminic style, Aayi helped me down from the cart. By the time we reached the back door of the buffalo-owner's house, the sun was scorching. I waited outside watching the she-buffalo. My aayi was speaking to a woman of the house.

"Hey, old woman,
have you brought enough fodder?"
"I have brought the fodder, yavva."
"How much have you brought?
Looks too little in your sari knot."
"No, yavva, it's two kilograms."
"Have you brought a man with you?
What is this? You have brought such a small boy!
Is he a hero to catch the buffalo?!"
"No, yavva ... how can he catch?
I am there and I will hold the buffalo myself.
You need not come at all.
You just bring the buffalo."

By that time, a man's voice was heard. Aayi started muttering to herself. The fellow who came out glanced at my aayi and the woman, and went inside saying something to the woman. She followed him into the house. After a while, he came out.

"Namasgari yappa," my aayi folded her hands in greeting.

"Hey old woman, didn't we tell you the last time,
we have got the buffalo castrated?
We no longer let him near a she-buffalo.
Didn't we tell you that we use him now for drawing water from the well?"

My aayi pleaded with him, but it was futile.

Aayi finally lost her patience. She seized the rope from my hand and banged the buffalo's hump with the cudgel. The buffalo started mooing, "*Hyaom-hyaom.*" The he-buffalo inside responded, "*Yaom-yaom.*" The animals began a conversation. The fellow had already closed the door and gone inside. Even as the she-buffalo tugged at the rope, my aayi held it tight so that she could not budge. Aayi once again punched our buffalo on the hump. The she-buffalo started running at such a speed that Aayi had to run with her. The people who had reared the he-buffalo had come to the front door, and seeing Aayi run, they burst into laughter. Aayi's voice synchronized with the buffalo's as she raced with her. Since I was left behind, I started crying out of fear. Aayi was running behind the buffalo and at the same time signalling me to follow her.

When I reached the tar road, both Aayi's tonal pitch and the buffalo's pace had gradually reduced. She started shouting angrily,

"I told you not to come, did you listen?
You run behind me desperately
as if Aayi is rushing off to eat laddu all alone!"
Later, she softened her voice and pacified me.
"Come on, run faster, why are you crying?"

Something else bothered Aayi now. If we returned home and headed for Basarkod, it would only mean more travel. If we went to Basarkod straight from Kuntoji, what about our empty bellies? The scorching sun was right over our heads. Though Aayi told me to go back home, I refused. I even assured her that I was not hungry and would be able to walk with her.

The journey continued. The tar road was burning our feet. We reached the road used by the carts. Aayi had given me her footwear. Sometimes there were unmatched slippers on Aayi's feet—the slipper on her left foot would be completely different from the one on the right. But this time, when I wore them, one was thick-soled and the other was flat. Aayi's feet were very large. My feet were not even half that size. When I walked with those slippers, they not only made a big *turr-burr turr-burr* noise, but kicked up dust all around. I felt like a lame horse. It was not possible to walk in those slippers for long. It was not the first time I was wearing such slippers. One would find them on my feet only while crossing the bunds in the field, and in places where there were thorns. Otherwise, they would be in my hands.

On reaching Basarkod, we saw cattle grazing in the barren fields and hills. Perhaps a buffalo among them welcomed our she-buffalo. Listening to her, our she-buffalo shook off her reins and started running. Aayi was right behind her. I was quite far from Aayi.

As Aayi went farther and farther away, my weeping reached its peak. For fear of losing my aayi, the slippers in my hand did not even reach my feet in spite of the thorns. My weeping intensified when the thorns pricked me. Aayi did not mind the she-buffalo sprinting away from her, she only wished there had been a male buffalo in the herd. But she was disappointed.

We stood near the backdoor of the desai's house with our she-buffalo. It seemed as if here too the servants played plenty of politics. What happened in Kuntoji's house was repeated here. The local proverb—no profit for the road taken—proved true. So we began our journey back home with the she-buffalo. Somebody must have told Aayi something then. Our route took a completely different turn. It was the path leading to desai's farm. We walked a little and waited there.

Several questions and answers revolved in our heads. The sun was going down. Darkness was spreading swiftly. The village cattle were homebound. Perhaps desai's cattle were starting from the farm towards their shed. The cattle walked past us. The she-buffalo was already beginning to get agitated. She started tugging at the rope. The he-buffalo among the cattle initiated the proposal. Our buffalo was trying hard to escape from the thick rope around her neck. Aayi started making a booing sound. All of a sudden our buffalo started running. Aayi's song reached a crescendo. The young man grazing the cattle looked at my aayi and then at his cattle. By then the he-buffalo had slipped out of his clutches.

Aayi took note of my weeping voice and started consoling me in a tone different from the earlier one. Aayi must have let go of the buffalo deliberately.

The she-buffalo ran faster. The he-buffalo that escaped from the young man's hand followed her at the same speed. Perhaps the young man did not want to run behind the he-buffalo leaving the other animals behind. Later, another fellow came and for sometime followed the two buffaloes. When it proved futile, he just stared at my aayi.

Even though it was getting dark, we made several trips between the desai's house and farm searching for our buffalo. But we did not spot her. We had no clue where she was. Finally we made our way back home, dragging our feet. When we woke up the next morning, our buffalo was in our backyard. With her was the desai's he-buffalo!

How can a society, which does not let even the creations of Vishwamitra make love naturally, give a chance for human lovers to meet? Which is why stories like that of Marammadevi and the buffalo have branched out so widely.

Translated from Kannada by Dharani Devi Malagatti, Janet Vucinich and N. Subramanya

DAMODAR MORE

Damodar More (1953–) did an M.A. in Marathi and has a degree in journalism. He currently heads the Department of Marathi at the Joshi Bedekar College in Thane. He has several poetry collections to his credit, and many of his poems have been translated into Hindi. This poem, featured first in the pioneering anthology Poisoned Bread *(1992), has been much cited and reproduced. "Poetry Reading" stresses the fact that a sympathetic and interested audience is essential to a writer—no one can speak to an empty hall.*

POETRY READING

As I was reading out a poem
the audience was listening as I read
And as the audience was listening to me
I was reading the faces of the audience.

As I continued to read…
There came a moment—who knows why—
when a couple of them wrinkled their noses
And astonished, I said to the poet in me
'What's the reason for this?'
And he answered me,
'It was to be expected…
All that's happened is
the settled sludge has been stirred
and the water's grown cloudy.'

As I was reading out a poem
the audience was listening as I read
And as the audience was listening to me

I was reading the faces of the audience.

As I continued to read…
There came a moment when
a couple got up and left
But the eyelids of the others
seemed ready to shed rain
And, distressed, I said to the poet in me,
'Why is this happening?'
And he answered me,
'It's only natural
All that's happened is
the moisture pent up till today
is looking to break out.'

As I was reading out a poem
the audience was listening as I read
And as the audience was listening to me
I was reading the faces of the audience.

As I continued to read…
There came a moment when
I saw embers flaring in the pupils of their eyes
And, frightened, I said to the poet in me,
'What's this that's happening?'
And he answered me,
'It was this I was waiting for
All that's happening is
the dynamite fuses, nearly burnt out,
are trying to flare up again.'

As I was reading out a poem
the audience was listening as I read
And as the audience was listening to me
I was reading the faces of the audience.

As I continued to read…
There came a moment when

I saw a dazzling brilliance in their eyes
And, curious, I said to the poet in me,
'Why is this happening?'
And he answered me,
'It's inevitable.
All that's happening is
they're marching in battle
on this fearful darkness.'

As I was reading out a poem
the audience was listening as I read
And as the audience was listening to me
I was reading the faces of the audience.

Translated from Marathi by Priya Adarkar

AJAY NAVARIA

Born in Delhi, Ajay Navaria (1972–) is the author of two collections of short stories, Patkatha aur Anya Kahaniyan *(2006) and* Yes Sir *(2012), and a novel,* Udhar ke Log *(2008). He has been associated with the premier Hindi literary journal,* Hans. *Navaria teaches in the Hindi department at Jamia Milia Islamia University, Delhi.* Unclaimed Terrain *(2013), a collection of his short stories translated into English, has been critically acclaimed.*

NEW CUSTOM

The man's nostrils quivered, blasted by stench. As soon as he alighted from the bus, his nose collided with the smell, while his eyes met the form of a man lying naked in the distance. Was there a relationship between the two? He thought about it for a moment, but it was hard to make a connection because the odour—whether of rotting flesh or soured milk—was coming from the opposite direction.

The bus stand was quite deserted. The wind was exceedingly cold; the man shivered despite his warm coat. Of their own, his hands sought out the warmth of his trouser pockets, only to quickly re-emerge to tighten his rust-colored muffler. Romila had insisted on wrapping it around his neck as he left, the same way she sometimes put her arms lovingly around him. His conscience stirred, and he wondered why he was always in a fault-finding mood with her. It depressed him.

He wanted to wrap the muffler around his ears—it would surely have brought him some relief—but he couldn't. People who wore mufflers around their ears were looked down on in the city; he would be jeered at with shouts of "Hey Bihari! Oye Bihari!" which was yet another way of making people feel inferior. He preferred suffering the piercing wind to being branded a muffler-bundled Bihari.

It was well past nine in the morning, but because of the heavy fog, it seemed like night was gathering. The sun's rays could not penetrate the dense fog. There was just enough illumination to see as far as one's hands, but it was a drowsy light, not a lively one. A damp gleam was settling in all directions as though a big furry brown cat had stretched itself out.

There were only a few days left for spring, but this year the winter had shown no sign of relenting. All the newspapers and TV channels said the cold this season had broken a thirty-year record—the Meteorological Department's forecast had been proved wrong once again—and, interspersed with dispirited offerings of 'chewing-gum news', the channels were packed with ads for various national and international products to keep you from the cold. In one, a slender, beautiful girl hides her boyfriend from her father in a large fridge, where he is discovered happily eating ice cream. The cold doesn't bother him in the least because he wears the thermal undergarments the advertiser is promoting. A rival manufacturer shows how a young girl's devotion to a flabby old man causes his youthful nephew much heartache, upon which the man vainly and indecently leers that it is an 'inside' matter. A tonic advertisement features honeymooners raving about a saffron-containing product and the 'heat' it generates. This is a man's world, where women are treated like objects and men are deluded into believing themselves to be the consumers. In this game, it is hard to know who the product is and who the customer; everyone is stirred around in the same pot.

If he lowered his eyes a bit, they snagged on the naked man again. Was he dead? The question smouldered. He picked up his suitcase and walked in the man's direction. He stared straight ahead.

"Take a seat, darbar," a voice broke his reverie.

A man at a roadside tea stall was watching him as he set an aluminum pot on a big stove. The stove was fired up and emitted a low, hissing sound, its flames making the blackened pot even blacker. The wayfarer shifted his attention from the pot with effort, his glance transfixed instead by a big chunk of fresh ginger lying on some greasy sacks near the man's fat, filthy feet.

Inwardly, he smiled when the shopkeeper called him 'darbar'. The man knew that this form of address was reserved for the thakur landlords of the region. Perhaps the shopkeeper had assumed him to be one, going by his tall stature and broad frame. Or was it his thick moustache? Or perhaps it was a marketing strategy to flatter potential customers. But then why would a customer be gratified at being called 'darbar'?

"Tea," said the traveller, surprising himself. Given how filthy the place was, how could he drink tea here? His own voice sounded alien to him. At home, he upbraided Romila for kneading dough without washing her hands after closing the bathroom door—a comparatively small matter. Romila's retort was that she had already washed her hands with soap in the bathroom washbasin, so why the fuss?

"You don't care for hygiene!" he would shout to cover his discomfiture. "And you're obsessed with cleanliness!" she would squawk like a chicken in a coop.

The shopkeeper crushed some ginger and put it in the black water seething in the even blacker pot.

"I shouldn't watch this," he thought and looked in the other direction. After all, he wanted to drink tea. Having taught for ten years at a famous university in the metropolis, he had acquired a special kind of pride and refinement. A short distance away from this stall was another, and then a third and a fourth, each with small black pots mounted on black stoves.

There were two puppies at the opposite stall that were keeping warm by wrestling each other. This entertained him, and he began to take an interest. The brown puppy, who was a little skinny but extremely feisty, sometimes pulled the white puppy's ear, or bit his tail, or stuck his teeth into his neck. The white pup was plump and dignified, and had a long mark like a saffron tilak on his forehead. He ran a little distance, whining *kuun-kuun ghoon-ghoon*, but then he got annoyed, flipped the skinny brown pup over, and stood on him. Some devout soul had tried to erase the difference between the two by putting a saffron tika on the brown puppy's forehead as well, but it was very light, and you could only see it if you looked hard enough.

Across the way, their mother lay dozing.

"Here you are, darbar," the shopkeeper's voice penetrated the man's intense concentration the way a spider enters its web, stalking its prey. When the shopkeeper repeated "Darbar, tea!" in a brisk voice, the man turned his attention toward him. The shopkeeper had a dusky, oily face that sported a vermilion tilak. His rotten teeth were stained black by paan masala. The man's attention moved to the streamers of poisonous paan masala and tobacco packets hanging in the shop.

"This is how the English turned the Chinese into opium addicts."

"What?" The shopkeeper could make no sense of the man's utterance.

"Nothing. So, how did you know…" he paused.

"What?"

"…that … I'm a darbar." He turned his gaze from the shopkeeper's face and took a sip.

"Oh, that's easy, darbar. Seeing your coat and pants, and your commanding presence, anyone would know," his voice was sycophantic.

"Are you one too?"

"No, not at all." He was embarrassed. "I'm a mali, darbar, a saini." His hands were joined as though seeking forgiveness.

The traveller turned his head and started to drink his tea. His attention once again turned toward the roughhousing puppies and their mother, who had now lifted her head and was taking pleasure in her pups' wrestling.

He recalled the conversation he'd had with his father the night before he left home. "No, even if you repeat it a hundred times, I still won't accept it … money changes everything … village, city, town … all of it." He saw his father's emotional upheaval. "You're wrong, thinking that we could ever live well without it." He rubbed his finger and thumb together, signifying hard cash. "Only with forbearance and piety—my foot! Is this so-called piety meant only for us?" He stamped angrily. "All these righteous souls crave worldly possessions, which only come from hard work and are bought with money."

"Still, be careful, everything is just as it was there … the change that money has wrought is the change you see on rocks in a river-bed." A father is anyway weakened in the face of a grown-up son. The position of a young, salaried son is like a young lion's. His father inevitably starts to quietly accept the new order, like an old lion must.

"No, Papa, money changes everything." His voice was firm.

"Hey, shoo! Get out of here!" The shopkeeper yelled, and the man snapped back to the present. The shopkeeper was chasing the puppies that had slipped under the tables set outside his stall.

"What's the population of this village?" he looked toward the shopkeeper.

"Which one? There are three villages, that's why this place is also called Tigaon, Tri-village. One is Vanla ki Dhani, then there is Raj-garh, and the third is Kiratgarh. Which one are you asking about?"

"Rajgarh."

"There are about three thousand houses ... there must be about twenty-five thousand people."

"Twenty-five thousand..." he gaped. "It's a pretty big village."

"Yes, darbar, they say that three or four hundred years ago, it was the biggest trading hub of the area ... now it's become a poor village." The shopkeeper put his hands on his knees and stood up, then stepped down from the stall. He drew a long bamboo pole from under the stall, hung a fat electrical wire on it, and attached it to the government power cable above the stall.

"What is this?" the man laughed.

"Connection..." The shopkeeper simply shrugged his shoulders, came back inside and squatted down as before. He reached for a portable television set lying at the back of the stall, brought it forward, and switched it on. An ad came on with an aged film actress making a living selling a brand of chips.

"Do you have those?" the man asked the shopkeeper, cocking an eyebrow at the screen.

"Which, the chips or the heroine?" the shopkeeper snickered. The man disliked his lascivious joke and laughter.

The shopkeeper read the disapproval in his face. "I have them!" He took down a basket hanging at the back of the stall, in which there were several kinds of chips—Kurkure, Bingo. "Can't stock everything up front." The shopkeeper hung the basket on a protruding nail at the entrance to his stall.

"There's mineral water too," he gestured toward the bottled water arranged there and muttered, "Have you come to see the fort?" The shopkeeper was inclined to chat. In this cold, he didn't have any other customers. The man was the only traveller to get off the bus here.

The shopkeeper's question went unheard. On the television set, an international channel was now showing pictures of Saddam Hussein. American soldiers had arrested him in a bunker and were interrogating him, forcing him to open his mouth. The channel showed this scene over and over. America was making him an example to the world, issuing a warning of how they would similarly go after anyone who crossed them.

"You've come to see the fort, darbar?" The shopkeeper repeated his question.

"No, I've come for a wedding." He took a sip of tea.

"At whose place?" The question got trapped in his eyebrows, the way a fly thrashes about when it is caught in someone's hair.

"Dharm Singhji's place." The man straightened his back.

"Oh, I see, I had no idea there was a wedding at the darbar saheb's place." He struck his forehead with his hand theatrically. "Darbar saheb, my wife is right when she says I am so wrapped up in my work that I have no idea what's going on around me. Now, you tell me, what's a man to do? I leave the house in the morning and come back late at night. I slave away the whole day for two pieces of roti ... and what do women do? They live off our earnings, they idly eat and sleep. On top of this, they complain, 'We have to do the cooking. If you'd have to cook you'd know.' I tell you..."

He stopped for a moment and started again. "Believe me, when his elder daughter was married, I slogged real hard ... I was young then." He twirled his moustache. "I even gave five cots and eight copper pots for the wedding party's stay ... my whole family slept on the ground for five days ... I mean, why not? After all, she's the daughter of the village. Her honour is ours ... you have to think of every little detail."

"Hmm." The man was staring determinedly at the TV and trying to shut out the shopkeeper's chatter.

"You have to maintain the rules and customs of the village," the shopkeeper jabbered on.

"Hmm," said the man downing the last of his tea and putting the glass on the table.

"Dharm Singhji hasn't said a word about his daughter getting married," the shopkeeper muttered quietly. "How strange."

"Not his daughter, his son." The man took out a handkerchief and wiped his mouth.

"His son?" The question shot up through his eyebrows. "Which Dharm Singhji are you talking about?"

"Dharm Singhji of Rajgarh," the man's voice was soaked in indifference.

"But he doesn't have a son. God only gave the poor man two daughters," the shopkeeper's voice was clammy with sorrow.

"Arrey, no, it's his son's wedding ... the wedding party will go to Jivangarh tomorrow ... today is the bhat, the rice ceremony." This time the man's voice had a glimmer of apprehension. He was hoping he wasn't in the wrong place.

"You've got it wrong somehow." There was harshness, conviction, and authority in the shopkeeper's voice. "Not just Dharm Singhji, I know the entire village. There must be a mix-up."

"Doesn't he work in the water-works department?" The man got irritated.

"Oh no! You're talking about Dharma Harijan, the operator," the shopkeeper slapped his forehead. "As if there could be a wedding in the village without my knowing!" The shopkeeper's voice was distant and rude.

"How much do I owe you?" Noting the shift in the shopkeeper's tone, the man pulled out a hundred-rupee note.

"Three rupees. But, brother, first wash the glass." This in the shopkeeper's rudest tone yet.

"Why?" The man felt as though a bucket of water had been dumped on him. His own voice seemed to come from the bottom of a well.

"Why?! This is the custom of the village," the shopkeeper shouted for any bystander to hear. "A rise in status does not put an end to custom."

The man stepped down from the stall. He suddenly thought of his father. He saw the naked man lying in the distance. He saw the puppies wrestling. A few people had gathered. It was as if he were naked among them. Their gaze scorched him.

"What's going on, Banwari?" a face from the crowd tossed out the question.

"See, Chaudhari, I had taken him to be a good man ... it's not as if it's written on someone's forehead who is what. He could have told me at the outset that he has come to Dharma Harijan's place," the shopkeeper answered rudely.

There was some hesitation among the bystanders when they saw the man's clothing and impressive stature. The shopkeeper's next question was meant to clinch the issue. "Should I serve you tea now in a harijan glass?"

"And if I hadn't told you...?" Under the weight of the insult, the words emerged with difficulty.

"If you hadn't said anything, the sin would have been on you. You don't drink from a cup once you've spotted a fly in it," the shopkeeper shouted, raising his hands.

"Why are you being stubborn, brother? Just wash it, this is the custom here," a man came forward.

"Why make an issue of it?" another asked.

"Do you wash it too?" He turned toward the voice and asked haughtily.

"Why should I?" The man was offended.

"So then why should I?" came the retort.

"He's going to get thrashed. The bastard's exposed." The shopkeeper's war cry was not lost on the man.

"How much for this glass?" His jaw clenched in anger.

"Why?" The shopkeeper was surprised.

"Tell me how much it is." His brows were drawn together.

"Ten ... no, twenty rupees," the shopkeeper inflated the price.

"Take this," he thrust the hundred-rupee note at the shopkeeper. The father of the nation, Mahatma Gandhi, was smiling on the note, wrapped in a shawl. The shopkeeper quickly grabbed the money.

"Change." His eyebrows were stretched taut.

The man took the change from the shopkeeper, put it in his pocket. Picking up the glass, he smashed it against the chabutra, the platform under the trees on which village folk sat for tea and chit-chat. *Chanaak*—shards of glass flew in all directions. Startled by the noise, the mother dog jumped away, and the naked man suddenly sat up.

The man bent down, picked up his suitcase, and started toward the village. A smile bloomed on the shopkeeper's face, a smile not unlike Gandhiji's on the note.

Translated from Hindi by Laura Brueck

CHALLAPALLI SWAROOPA RANI

Born fourth in a family of five children, Challapalli Swaroopa Rani (1968–) studied history and archaeology while striving, simultaneously, to fill the gap she found in dalit feminist scholarship. Noting that dalit groups rarely pay any attention to issues of gender, and that feminism is of little use to dalits, her concern is to bring issues of caste, class and gender together. Swaroopa Rani published her first collection of poetry Mankenapuvvu (The Red Mankena Flower) in 2005 and has written for several little magazines and journals. She is currently associate professor in the Centre for Buddhist Studies, Nagarjuna University, Guntur.

WATER

Just as the water knows
the ground's incline,
it knows the generations-old strife
between the village and the wada.
Like the dampness on the well's edge that never dries,
it knows that untouchability never disappears.

The water knows everything.

It knows the difference of race
between the Samaria woman and Jesus the Jew.
It also knows the sub-caste difference
between leather and spool.

It knows the agony of the panchama,
who, not having the right to draw a pot of water,
waits all day near the well
with his empty pot
until a shudra arrives.

It knows the humiliation
of the wada girl
when he who poured the water from a distance,
falls all over and touches her.

It knows the righteous rage
of Karamchedu Suvarthamma[1]
who opposed the kamma landlords
with her water pot
when they asked her not to pollute the pond water.

The water is witness
to centuries of social injustice.

When I see water
I remember
how my wada would thirst all day
for a glass of water.

For us, water is not simply H_2O,
for us, water is a mighty movement.
It is the Mahad struggle at the Chavadar tank.
A single drop of water embodies
tears shed over several generations.

In the many battles we fought
for a single drop of water,
our blood flowed like streams.
But we never managed to win
even a small puddle of water.

When I see water,
I remember
how we welcomed our weekly bath
as if it was a wondrous festival!

---

[1] Suvarthamma's raising of her water pot (to ward off the knife that was thrown at her) was taken as an offence and was the ostensible reason for the kammas going on a rampage, killing over a dozen dalits in Karamchedu in 1985.

While the entire village bathed luxuriously—
twice a day.

When I see water
I remember
my childhood,
when we walked miles
to reach the big canal
and carried back heavy pots,
with the muscles and veins on our necks straining, bursting.

I remember,
its thatched roofs aflame,
the malapalle burning to ashes
for want of a pot of water.

Water is not a simple thing!
It can give life
but it can also devour lives.
The water that refused to quench parched throats
became the killer tsunami wave,
that swallowed whole,
village after village.
The poor are but playthings
in its vicious hands.
Often, it turns villages into dry deserts
and sometimes it drowns them in floods.

Between the village and the wada
between one state and another,
this water can ignite many struggles and strife.
It can make the blood run in streams.
but it can also sit innocently
in a Bisleri bottle.

This water from our village well
that forces us to do many a circus feat,
now slowly, surreptitiously,

dances its way into the Pepsi man's bottle.
With its new name 'mineral water'
it takes to the skies,
it raises a storm.

Now
water is no mean matter.
It's a multinational market commodity.

As they say
water is omniscient.
It contains the world.

Translated from Telugu by Uma Bhrugubanda

RAGHAVAN ATHOLI

Raghavan Atholi (1957–) is a poet, novelist and sculptor, whose sculptures in red laterite (traditionally used by stone-cutters and masons) have been exhibited across India. He has published five collections of poems—starting with Kandathi *in 1996—and a novel,* Choraparisham *(Bond of Blood, 2007), in Malayalam. His poetry, he tells us in this interview with Pradeepan Pampirikunnu, accesses a continent of lost words.*

THE POET WITH A FOREST FIRE INSIDE

Pradeepan Pampirikunnu: *Kandathi* is your first published collection of poems. Could you tell us a little about the circumstances of its publication?

Raghavan Atholi: I have always wanted to record the caste-related experiences and survival of the subordinated castes. Such a record would also be the record of my own life. I had been asking the Kerala government publication department since 1986 to publish the book. But they didn't do anything until 1996, after Geethanandan [leader, along with C.K. Janu, of the Adivasi Gothra Maha Sabha] and I approached Ayyappa Paniker [distinguished Malayalam poet] for a preface to the collection. Paniker not only wrote the preface, but also got it published in the signature series, *Keralakavitha*.

PP: Could you talk about the poetic language used in *Kandathi*?

RA: For some years before I wrote the poems in *Kandathi*, I had been experimenting with rhythms and trying to bring some of that into my poetry. The aim was to create an intense beat that lies between prose and poetry; an effort to become the rhythm of my people—a rhythm that also provides the energy for their hard work. It is not a rhythm to sit still and reflect upon. Poetry, for me, is not the worship of beauty either.

PP: There's also a certain note of lament in your poetry. Is that part of this rhythm?

RA: Poetry is both lament and uproar. In my case, it is also a process of identifying with subordinated people all over the world; an awareness of our oneness. That is how the thread of nationalism develops in this poetry—as a universal brotherhood of communities, including black people.

PP: It is generally accepted that emotions welling up from real life are characteristic of dalit poetry and that your poetry is emotional. What is the basis for the emotionalism in your poetry?

RA: So far, no one has ever asked me about poetry, let alone about the nature of its emotion. Well, no one actually thought that we had a life to speak of! I feel that in any given period, someone is entrusted to give expression to the form and feeling of the time. The sorrows and problems that have been left unspoken for centuries, the people who've been denied a voice to talk about them—it is for them that I lament, that I scream. The souls of our ancestors come back through art forms like theyyam. They shriek, they cry. Inside me I have the lament of our ancestors as well as the sorrows of our contemporaries. When I write, they sit beside me, and I forget myself and my surroundings. Poetry, for me, is neither complaint nor salvation. It is a historical commitment.

PP: Do you think there is a difference between this emotion and the sentimentality of the romantics?

RA: The emotion in my poetry is a living heritage. It is not based on either completely spiritual or completely material emotions. It is based on emotions that have been formed entirely by social humiliation, experiences of caste, poverty. Yes, they are entirely different from the sentimentality of the Malayalam romantics.

PP: Do you consider folk songs the foundation for subaltern poetry? Have you tried to purposely bring the beauty, rhythms and patterns of these songs and their music into your poetry?

RA: My writing comes through my unconscious mind, thus providing a passage for generations. I'm only an agent, a cause. The rhythms are already there, as in the songs that my mother sings. That is why I gave my first collection her name—Kandathi. "All the leisure literature of the landlords does not add up to a single exhalation from my mother," I once said.

PP: Are you critical of the Malayalam poetic tradition?

RA: There is only one poetry—for the entire universe. I can only be part of that. The current context has some specific demands and that is what creates dalit poetry. I have no objection to a poetic tradition. But I insist on knowing how it was produced: the present tradition was created by copying and taking over my ancestors' songs and words. The task today is to re-possess those words. Remember, in the whole body of Sangam literature only one brahmin is found.

PP: But Malayalam poetry follows the lineage of Sanskrit literature and not that of Sangam literature—don't you agree?

RA: Even before the Sangam period, there were rhythms—of the one who cut wood, the one who harvested the paddy fields, the one who pound the paddy. These are not upper-caste or upper-class rhythms. Aristocratic experiences have been sneaked into these rhythms and songs. What I feel is that we have to re-capture these primordial rhythms. My tradition is that of the original, primordial man.

PP: Is it possible to divide Malayalam poetry into upper caste and untouchable (savarna and avarna)?

RA: Of course! But even in this division, a brotherhood has to be possible between them. One tradition cannot or should not stifle the other. The contemporary tradition of Malayalam poetry is one of a people with no experience. Which upper-caste person has the experience of cultivating paddy fields? How many children have they lost to poverty and hunger? Do the upper-caste people have such experiences? No. What we call 'dalit' is not the experience of one person, but of a whole humanity. In other words, there is no need to name poetry as 'dalit poetry' or 'Malayalam poetry'. It is the upper caste that names it in this way. The names they give represent their experiential realm. We have no authority. We have to develop an authority as a people, become a significant political force. We have to recognize our own voices, our own languages, mark our songs and art. This will be a process of marking another kind of nationalism.

PP: Is caste the principal force in your poetry? If you did not belong to this caste, would you be writing poetry?

RA: When I write, there is no caste in me. Poetry is my mother tongue. My people are my language. What I do is establish them in my poetry. I don't know if that constitutes caste. Kandathi, Chathan, Aritheyi are all in my poems because they are the ones who form my poetic consciousness.

Their centrality in my experiences is of course due to our shared caste. What I have seen is their lives and their troubles. Whatever I write, I come back to them. When I write, I'm not concerned whether this constitutes dalitness. I am concerned whether this constitutes poetry.

PP: What are your thoughts when your poetry is marked out as dalit poetry?

RA: I don't think I write dalit poetry. I am a dalit and I write universal poetry.

PP: Could you explain that a little?

RA: I don't think my poetry is to be confined to Kerala or even India. It is for everyone around the world. That is what I mean by universal poetry.

PP: But such an idea of the universal runs the risk of silencing the regional and the national, surely?

RA: No. What I mean by nationalism is a shared identity of oppressed communities. Oppressed groups all around the world constitute a 'nation'. It is from this point of view that I envision my poetry as universal.

PP: Sharan Kumar Limbale has said: "What is important to me is not the word, but the pain and sorrow that it represents." Do you see language as important in your poetry?

RA: The dalit has a mother tongue. But he cannot talk to the larger society in it—there is no space for his language there. So he has to use written Malayalam. Dalits are people who were denied the freedom of movement by day. So they spoke in a different language. Panan, parayan, mannan—all of them have their own language. We have not been able to bring any of that into poetry. Not just poetry—

the possibilities embedded in those languages have not been explored by Malayalam. There is a whole continent of lost words there.

PP: Then who do you write for in Malayalam?

RA: The poetry that I write is for the whole world. I do try to use the language of my clan when possible. My novel *Choraparisham* is an attempt to use the language of our caste. I don't have the authority to tell you to read or listen to my poetry. I believe that I have a share in all the beauty and narration in this world—I am part of a people who have produced that world. I will use everything that my society has created as an instrument for the progress of my community.

PP: Do you see a weakness in the 'new poetry' in Malayalam?

RA: New poetry has not succeeded in bringing today's society and times into poetry or poetry into today's times. They think poetry is a solitary experience. Not for me. As I write, an entire community comes surging in...

PP: Kandan, Kandathi, Eyilandi, Arippandi, Kariyathan, Vellayyi—you have used several names from oppressed communities as titles for your poems. What was your intention here?

RA: There are multitudes of books and not one of them has people from my community. I believe that there is a need to inscribe them. I believe that to be my assignment as a poet. All I am doing is to verbalize the inner agitation of a people who have been silenced for so long.

PP: The communists in Kerala have upheld poetry as social resistance. They have also seen themselves as representing oppressed people. But they have never considered you as a communist poet. The progressive literary movement has also not given much attention to your work. Why do you think this is?

RA: I have written a poem titled "Brahminism". It deals with the casteist underpinnings of communism. In India, this has been formed by an alliance between brahmins and communists. They see those of us who raise the issue of caste as enemies. They have been blind to caste and to people like us who have been forced to live the oppressions of caste.

PP: In the poem "Thanichirippaval" (Alone She Sits) you wrote:

Black woman
Become poetry, and
Sting my body.

Ayyappa Paniker called his preface to your book 'the aesthetics of blackness'. What do you understand as the aesthetics of blackness?

RA: 'Black' is a powerful symbol that overcomes even the national boundaries of the possibility of the word 'dalit'. My heart pulsates when I hear Jackson sing. Blackness is a representational term that unifies oppressed people the world over. That's why it occupies so much space in my poetry.

PP: What is your appraisal of the poet Raghavan Atholi?

RA: I don't think I am a poet yet. On the primordial grasslands of my people, there is poetry. I might yet become a poet when I get there. That will be my true poetry.

Translated from Malayalam by Jayasree Kalathil

T.M. YESUDASAN

T.M. Yesudasan (1953–) was born to Christian parents of dalit origin at a time when the Left movement in Kerala was mushrooming. He was an active participant in several movements to rid the church of the hierarchy created between dalits and Syrian Christians. Yesudasan has been the editor of two historically significant little magazines: Yuvalokam *(1983) and* Dynamic Action *(1988–89). He taught for several years in the English Department of* CMS *college, Kottayam and retired as head of the department in 2008. In 1992, he sought to articulate the dilemma between the relevance of the Left and scepticism about it in the context of caste, through a series of lectures in Kuruchi; "Towards a Prologue to Dalit Studies" was the first in the series.*

TOWARDS A PROLOGUE TO DALIT STUDIES

Introduction

Conditions are ripe today for the 'outbreak' of dalit studies. Everywhere it is the aborigines/indigenous peoples who are subjected to the most inhuman kind of oppression and exploitation. The notion of oppressed, indigenous nationalities/minorities and a growing awareness of the racist/casteist core of the dominant classes emerge from this pan-indigenous fact of oppression. Dalit consciousness and dalit studies have their roots in this growing awareness of savarna supremacy or casteism.

All over the world the oppressed social groups, considered inferior 'others', are at present engaged in serious explorations of history and interrogations of culture. This is part of an attempt to retrieve lost pride and honour with the intention of redefining their sense of self. The desire is not to be lost in past grandeur, but to understand the problems of the day and to work towards a more humane future of the world. In this era of the third-wave civilization,[1] at a time when the

---

[1] Alvin Toffler, *The Third Wave* (New York: Bantam Books, 1984).

present is fast receding into history, the oppressed classes raise certain self-reflexive questions: do we have a role to play in the ever-changing scenario in which history and the future are both fast evolving? Will social invisibility and political powerlessness continue to haunt our destiny, leaving us in perpetual wretchedness and humiliation? Dalit studies originates on the premises of these disturbing questions and frustrations of the people.

One of the lessons we learn from history is that only a people who initiate a politics of self-representation[2] and maintain records of their discursive practices will find a place in history and culture. Dalit studies, therefore, is a political mode of enquiry and explanation generating discourses on the past, present and future of dalits in order to help them find a place in history and culture and shape their future.

It is rather difficult to find ready acceptance and recognition for dalit studies in a savarna society entrenched in classical aesthetics and cultural norms. But it is possible through the collective political and intellectual endeavour of the entire dalit community to open channels of dialogue with civil society. It is this belief that prompted this paper, which, in fact, is not the prologue that dalit studies deserves. Mine is simply an exercise embryonic in form in search of directions, a groping in the dark for something to grasp. I solemnly place this embryonic utterance in this matrix of dalit activists and intellectuals with the earnest hope that they will develop the discourse to its fullness and rigour, helping it to come of age and find its destiny.

Breaking Out

In our academies, the production and distribution of knowledge goes through various procedures of rigorous social control. This process is called the politics of knowledge: to choose from a large body of information available, leave the rest out, subject the select knowledge to editing and interpreting, confer on it scientificity and objectivity, reduce its availability and limit its accessibility. In the academic assembly line, knowledge is produced by passing through these epistemo-

---

[2] Karl Marx and Friedrich Engels, *Selected Works in Three Volumes*, (Moscow: Progress Publishers, 1977), vol. 1, 479. Ambedkar's demand for separate electorate was meant to assert dalit self-representation.

logical procedures of social control.[3] What is always left out in these ideological apparatuses of the state[4] is the history and knowledge of the oppressed. It is the voice of the broken which is always silenced. It is the truth of the oppressed which is always excluded. The task of dalit studies is to release the counter-hegemonic forces of critique in order to facilitate the eruption of dalit voice and truth, breaking the silence and darkness in the midst of the prevailing politics of knowledge. Outbreak or eruption is entirely a conception of the people. This is possible only through the collective political and intellectual outburst of the entire community.

Dalit studies concerns itself with all aspects of dalit experience which, contrary to the views perpetrated and obstinately maintained by the upper castes, is complex, various, vast and rich. It engages dialectically with history, economics, political science, sociology, social psychology, literature, art, aesthetics, media studies, ecology and feminism; in fact, with all the major branches of social and human sciences. It also runs parallel to and crisscrosses the whole gamut of human knowledge from the theory of evolution to the science of eugenics.

Objectives

The objectives of dalit studies roughly are: to retrieve dalit traditions and forms of knowledge and subject them to analysis and interpretation; to examine the causes of dalit 'backwardness' and related issues; to develop dalit perspectives on the past, present and future of the world; and, to formulate dalit categories and concepts for critical analysis and interpretation. However, these objectives are in no way comprehensive; they are rather provisional, sketchy and tentative, open to addition, deletion and emendation.

Contexts

It is said that nothing comes out of nothing. There are certain social

---

[3] Michel Foucault, "The Order of Discourse," trans. Ian McLeod, in R. Young ed., *Untying the Text: A Poststructuralist Reader* (Boston: Routledge and Kegan Paul, 1981), 48–78.

[4] Louis Althusser, "Ideology and Ideological State Apparatuses," in *Lenin and Philosophy and Other Essays*, trans. Ben Brewster (Monthly Review Press, 1971).

and historical contexts that facilitate the emergence of a new science or discipline. This determinate social and historical context that makes the attitude of a new science audible and visible is what Husserl calls the 'life-world' (lebenswelt). Dalit studies evolved under the following limiting conditions emerging at global and national levels, which have a bearing on the everyday practices of dalit life-worlds.

Caste and casteism

Every society offers an explanation for its structure. The explanation given by Indian society is that of the caste system. There appears to be no reason to challenge Kosambi's view that the most important distinguishing feature of Indian society is jati or caste.[5] The word 'jati' indicates that Indian society has been divided on the basis of a self-consciousness which was either forcibly imposed upon or voluntarily chosen by a social group on the basis of birth, kinship, occupation or order of settlement. Caste becomes casteism when these social divisions are arranged in a hierarchical order and one's position in the hierarchy is used as justification for preferential treatment in intergroup relations.[6] Those higher in the hierarchy grab the monopoly of purity, ownership and control over the means of production and political power. Those in the lower strata become subservient to the upper classes. For instance, even now, most of those doing manual labour in the agricultural sector are drawn from certain castes customarily forced to the fields for centuries.[7]

Casteism has played an important role in devising the grammar of our language and designing the inflection of our behaviour. When individuals of higher and lower castes interact, signs of caste hierarchy become evident in their body language, choice of words and forms of address. There is no honorific in our language to refer to or address lower-caste people.[8] The upper castes have a monopoly over

---

[5] D.D. Kosambi, *The Culture and Civilization of Ancient India in Historical Outline* (New Delhi: Vikas, 1970), 15.

6 Paul Lehmann, *The Transfiguration of Politics: Jesus Christ and the Question of Revolution* (London: SCM Press, 1974), 164.

[7] M. Kunhaman, *Keralathinte Vikasanaprathisandhi* [Kerala's Development Crisis], (Thiruvananthapuram: CISRS, 1990), 13.

[8] Pierre Bourdieu, *The Logic of Practice* (London: Polity Press, 1992), 66–79.

all honorifics. These *micro-aggressions* affecting individual self-respect of dalits are as damaging as the *macro-aggressions* inflicted on a whole people,[9] for instance, the massacre of thirteen dalits on 6 August 1991 at Chunduru, Andhra Pradesh. When the pronoun *nee* (the familiar form of 'you') is removed from the Malayalam language, the social status of dalits will shoot up dramatically.

New casteism

New casteism refers to the phenomenon or tendency of denying or delaying justice to the traditionally oppressed social groups by adopting measures and positions which are ostensibly radical and progressive. The best example of this is the land reforms implemented in Kerala which gave farming land only to tenants, all of whom were upper castes. Dalits were barred from becoming tenants since they were slaves.[10] The land reforms of Kerala, by refusing to give farming land to dalits, reduced them to the condition of Choma, the eponymous character in the Kannada novel, *Chomante Thudi* or *Choma's Drum* (1938), by K. Shivarama Karanth. Choma, a pulaya, wants to own some land and become a farmer on his own, but no one in the village will give him a piece of land for cultivation as they believe that if a dalit owned land and became a farmer it would bring destruction on the village.[11]

The Kerala Land Relations Act of 1957 betrayed the same caste prejudice as that of the villagers in Karanth's novel. It did not take into account the fact that dalits were prevented from becoming tenants by caste and slavery against their will. Thus, dalits, the real tillers of the land, were given only house sites of three to ten cents. This injustice was done and was legitimized using the revolutionary *concept* of class, philosophically bracketing the *truth* of caste, and in the process achieving the victory of *method* over *truth*. Class perspective defined dalits as agricultural workers who have only their labour to sell and, therefore, have no claim to any kind of property. Workers

---

[9] Terms borrowed from Chester Pierce, a Harvard psychiatrist.

[10] Though slavery was abolished in Travancore in 1855, slaves continued to serve the same masters under the same conditions till the mid-twentieth century.

[11] K. Shivarama Karanth, *Chomante Thudi* (Choma's Drum) translated into Malayalam by K.V. Kumaran, (Trichur: Kerala Sahitya Akademi, 1978), 25.

are workers and are not supposed to be proprietors.

It is a pity that this land reform, one of the most unfair legislations vis-à-vis dalits, is acclaimed the world over as the most revolutionary. What is revolutionary for the upper castes is oppression for dalits. But, who are dalits to contradict the judgement of the whole world? As to matters of taste and judgement, dalits have no authority. One of the motivations driving dalit studies is the recovery of this authority denied by savarna domination. Similarly, take the case of the response of the Left parties when dalit members of Parliament demanded that a dalit be elected the president of India. The Left parties rejected the demand and defended their class image declaring that there should be no caste consideration in electing the president of India.

New brahminism or Hindutva

Brahminism, one of the oldest and most virulent colonial ideologies of the world, is being revived in the name of patriotism and nationalism. In politics, it takes the form of Hindutva, the Indian version of neo-Nazism. One of the reasons for the revival of brahminism as Hindutva is the emergence of backward castes and dalits as political forces to be reckoned with. In the social field, neo-brahminism incarnates itself as the anti-reservation struggle and the call for income-based reservations. In the field of culture, it fascinates the masses by projecting the dominant Hindu tradition as the Indian tradition in the print and electronic media; by mobilizing signs to produce privileged objects of culture for the savarnas who make them the focus of their identity and social relations. It is interesting to note how the telecast of *Mahabharata* and *Ramayana* re-imagined modern India as a primordial construct. Hindutva holds sway in domestic and foreign policies in the form of an increasing intolerance towards non-Hindu cultures and towards languages other than Hindi.[12]

---

[12] Krishna Kumar, "Hindu Revivalism and Education in North-Central India" *Social Scientist* 18 (October 1990): 4–26; Sukumar Muralidharan, "Mandal, Mandir aur Masjid: Hindu Communalism and the Crisis of the State" *Social Scientist*, 18 (October 1990): 27–49; Nancy Armstrong and Leonard Tennenhouse eds., *The Violence of Representation* (London: Routledge, 1989); Benedict Anderson, *Imagined Communities* (London: Verso, 1991).

The collapse of Gandhian integration and paternalism

The Gandhian dream of integration and the thesis of sanskritization did not work in the case of dalits. The hope that they will eventually merge with the Hindu community has been shattered. Dalit identity continues to be inassimilable in both sacred and secular spaces. Dalits who assert themselves and try to hold their heads high are subjected to defamation or incarceration on framed charges. Unable to withstand caste oppression in Hinduism, dalits choose to embrace Islam and Christianity in large numbers,[13] fully knowing that they will forfeit their Scheduled Castes privileges. For example, in 1981, about four hundred dalits in Madurai South district and a thousand at Meenakshipuram in Tirunelveli district of Tamil Nadu converted to Islam. Christianity in India is not a European religion, but a dalit path of Indian revolution. That is why Buddhism which went into exile in the medieval period, when savarna domination became intolerant and entrenched, is returning now in the form of Ambedkarian struggle. Gandhian paternalism and hegemony loses its power when dalits recognize it as a form of savarna domination.

The failure of Nehruvian centralism and the fall of Russian Socialism

The world has been witnessing a series of events that confirm the resilience of capitalism and the decline of socialism. The experiences of the Soviet republics and East European countries testify to this. Socialism failed to present a democratic model in those countries. It was the fascist models of socialism that collapsed. All fascisms are similar in eroding the diversity of peoples, in denying equality to different sections and in keeping the minorities under constant oppression. The case of Nehruvian centralism in India was not very different. The role played by this centralism in breaking down the federalism of the Indian nation state and the internal democracy of the ruling party and in undermining the democratic rights of the constitutive nationalities of the Indian Union was enormous. The Nehru dynasty cannot wash itself clean of the guilt of dismissing the popular government in Kerala in 1959. Nehruvian policies, marked by centralized planning,

---

[13] E.D. Devadason, *A Study on Conversion and its Aftermath* (Madras: CLS, 1982), 15 and 30.

bureaucracy and monopolies, effectively handed over the constitutive nationalities into the hands of the north Indian bourgeoisie and the brahmin lobby. The civil struggles taking place in India today are to a great extent the result of this Nehruvian centralism.

Oppressed indigenous peoples

The destitution of the indigenous people and the morbidity of the environment are interlinked and are the result of the subjection and exploitation of natural resources. The adivasis of Kerala, divested of their control over natural resources by the settlers from central Kerala, were forced to depend ultimately on their exploiters for survival. The dalit experience of the indigenous people begins with their alienation from their habitats. Even now, in 'enlightened' Kerala, the deprivation and displacement of the indigenous people is a continuing process. Books like *Keralatthile Africa* (The Africa in Kerala) and *Keralatthile America* (The America in Kerala), both written by K. Panoor, underline this gruesome tragedy. Oppressed indigenous people the world over are at the turning point of self-realization, because they have been gripped by the fear that there will never be a tomorrow if they continue to sit, like Mahabali, with their heads bowed before Vamana. Mahabali, the just and generous asura (indigenous) king, was treacherously deprived of his kingdom and murdered by the savarna god Vishnu disguised as a dwarf brahmin mendicant called Vamana who sought and received from the king a grant of three feet of land. With his two feet, Vamana measured the whole universe and put his third step on his benefactor's head. After trampling Mahabali on the head, and grinding him to the ground, Vamana breaks out into a eulogy of his victim's nobility and generosity. This myth may also offer the key to the Western anthropological notion of the 'noble savage', a strategic fiction which conceals the sly brutality of savarna domination.

Dalit consciousness

Being at the same time a dalit and a citizen of savarna India produces what W.E.B. Du Bois calls *double consciousness*. Du Bois was referring to the condition of the Afro-Americans: 'One ever feels his twoness—an American, a Negro; two souls, two thoughts, two unreconciled strivings; two warring ideals in one dark body, whose dogged strength alone keeps it from being torn asunder.'[14] Double consciousness splits the dalit mentally and saps her self-respect. A people without self-respect can never dream of emancipation. A consciousness, similar to that of black consciousness, is imperative to overcome the double consciousness that grips the dalit's nerves completely. Black appears undignified when perceived from a white perspective. To evaluate black, black criteria need to be employed. Dalitness does not indicate any deficiency born of origin or absence of anything; it is the effect of savarna domination devaluing everything that is dalit. Dalit studies springs from dalit consciousness.

The resurrection of Ambedkar's thought

The relevance of the thought of Ambedkar—who fought a lifelong battle for the protection and right to self-determination of dalits—has increased in the Indian political context where the clamour for a *Hindu Rashtra* that denies cultural diversity is becoming louder and louder. Like the ghost of Caesar who pursued his assassins Brutus and Cassius, Ambedkar's thought has started shining forth increasingly. Ambedkar was convinced that caste was rooted in the Vedas and sastras, the sacred scriptures of the Hindus;[15] therefore, conversion to a non-Hindu religion was imperative for social mobility and for the annihilation of the caste system. He criticized class politics for ignoring the fact of caste; he highlighted caste in order to transcend caste. His mission was the creation of an enlightened India (prabuddha Bharat) constituted by people enjoying samata or equality, rather than by castes oppressed under inequalities.

The emergence of dalit intellectuals and academics

A committed group of dalits consisting of teachers, students and activists is making its presence felt within and outside academia. It is the emergence of a willing academic community that facilitates the appearance of dalit studies as a discipline. The old chalices in academia are inadequate for the new wine brewed from dalit stud-

[14] W.E.B. Du Bois, *The Souls of Black Folk* (Chicago: A.C. McClurg & Co., 1903).
[15] B.R. Ambedkar, *Annihilation of Caste* (Bangalore: Dalit Sahitya Akademi, 1987), 64.

ies. As a result, Ambedkar study circles and dalit study centres are cropping up all over the country. Remarkable are the contributions made by political fronts like SEEDIAN Service Society (1972), Indian Dalit Federation (1986), Adhasthitha Navothana Munnani (Front for the Advancement of the Oppressed, 1988–89); ecumenical research centres like Christian Institute for the Study of Religion and Society (CISRS), Bangalore; development agencies like Backward People's Development Corporation (BPDC), Thiruvalla; and Ambedkar Study Circle, Alappuzha, towards keeping alive an interest in dalit issues.

A New Discipline

A new discipline comes into being when space is found for new ideas and approaches. Such new fields of knowledge could either be off-shoots of existing disciplines or those that are not fully developed and lie scattered in various disciplines. Be that as it may, the progenitors of new disciplines have the responsibility to explain how these are different from the others. This is necessary in order to achieve academic recognition as a discipline.[16]

To begin with, dalit studies challenges the objectivity of knowledge and endorses the view that different belief systems and contradictory interpretations are possible.[17] The story of Abraham in the Old Testament is a case in point. The Jews believe that Abraham brought for sacrifice Isaac born to his wife from the same caste, while the Muslims believe it was Ismail born of a wife from a different caste. Considering the context of the dispute over succession, it can be seen that the Muslim version may be right. In the end, it is Hagar and her son who are thrown out into the desert. Whose version is true? That of those who perpetrate injustice or of those who are at the receiving end? Dalit studies aligns itself with the victims.

Secondly, dalit studies deviates from the mainstream perspective of Indian sociological studies. In the mainstream academic view, India is today in the post-colonial stage where 'post' tacitly means 'after'. According to the dalit view, we are living in the new brahminic era which is only a continuation of centuries-old brahminic colonial-

---

[16] Norman MacKenzie ed., *A Guide to the Social Sciences* (Mentor, 1966), 9.
[17] Ibid., 15.

ism. Dalits are the Fourth World within Third World India. Specific insights such as these constitute dalit studies. Even as we completely agree with Frantz Fanon's views on the destructive effect of white colonialism on the colonized,[18] we have to admit that it is the same white colonialism that opened the possibility of emancipation of dalits from under the feet of brahminic colonialism.

When the Europeans arrived in India, the condition of dalits was not worth comparing to that of the Africans before colonialism.

The African people had their cultural institutions and control over natural resources. When the whites came to India, dalits had nothing worth recording. Whatever cultural notions and institutions they possessed were either denied any scope of development or were totally distorted under savarna domination. All paths had been closed to them. All fruits were forbidden. The fact that it was *brahminic colonialism* that meted out the dalit experience to the indigenous people is central to dalit studies. This does not mean that dalit studies is blind to the challenges and threats of colonialism, neo-colonialism and imperialism. On the contrary, this is to show how dalit studies differs in orientation from Indian sociological studies and African studies.

References

Balakrishnan, P.K. *Jathivyavasthithiyum Keralacharithravum* [Caste System and Kerala History]. Kottayam: NBS, 1983.

Chentharassery, T.H.P. *Ayyankali*. Thiruvananthapuram: Prabhat Book House, 1979.

Chirakkarodu, Paul et al. ed., *Dalit Kavithakal: Oru Patanam* [Dalit Poetry: A Study]. Thiruvalla: CLS, 1992.

Jose, N.K. *Ayyankali*. Vaikom: Hobby Publishers, 1989.

Satchidanandan, K., ed., *Karutha Kavitha* [Black Poetry]. Vadakara: Darsana Granthavedi, 1982.

Translated from Malayalam by the author

---

[18] Frantz Fanon, *The Wretched of the Earth* (Penguin Books, 1963).

CHANDRA BHAN PRASAD

Chandra Bhan Prasad (1958–) is one of the significant post-Ambedkarite public dalit intellectuals. He is the first dalit to gain regular space in a national English daily: he has been writing a weekly column called 'Dalit Diary' since 1999, in The Pioneer. *He has, since, written for leading Hindi dailies and is a regular face on television channels. In 1991, he started the Dalit Shiksha Andolan in Uttar Pradesh. He is also the architect of the Bhopal Document of 2001 that sought to create opportunities beyond reservation for dalits. Having started with the Marxist-Leninist movement, Prasad today sees capitalism and neoliberalism as the means to neutralize caste. Here are two pieces from his 'Dalit Diary' column.*

UNTOUCHABILITY AND ITS 'HIDDEN' AGENDA

The previous Sunday was the first anniversary of the Dalit Diary. The column had first appeared on 4 April 1999. Our friends and well-wishers decided to organize an informal get-together, to be followed by dinner. We also decided to invite some of our varna friends, whom we had known for long, and who have been involved in some kind of activism. The list contained some friends who are secular by conviction, and yet progressive. During the course of inviting various friends, something very interesting happened. While speaking to a very dear friend mine, I insisted she stay for dinner as well. Since her place was far away from the place where we were to assemble, she had genuine reasons to leave early. But I was very keen that she stayed for dinner. I began throwing incentives.

I first assured that there was one guest coming from the same area, and he could drop her. Next, I said that she would have an opportunity to interact with a group of dalit intellectuals she may have not met. And then I threw the ultimate enticement—in a lighter vein—that she may find her first opportunity to dine in a dalit family in an informal occasion. This logic of mine, the final one, somewhat upset her. For the record, she is a wonderful person, loved and respected by all of us. She was an important activist in the JNU [Jawaharlal Nehru University] student movement of 1983, has been an active sympathizer of the radical-Left movement in the country, and above all, of civil liberties movements. Of late, she made a minor deviation in tilting towards the secular brigade. That apart, she has been with dalit movements all along, and therefore, she never expected me to make a statement which amounted to questioning her anti-varna/caste credentials.

She continued explaining: that during her tour of the countryside, she had dinned in innumerable homes belonging to the poor—mostly dalits—without ever thinking of caste and untouchability, not even in the wildest of her dreams. The discussion prolonged paving the way for newer ideas. Trying to legitimize the statement I had made earlier, I, without questioning her anti-caste credentials, began posing newer questions. I asked her, to try recollecting one incident where in a non-official/non-political, or in any informal assembly at her home, in other words, in her day-to-day life, was there a dalit on her guest-list, and if she was on a dalit's similar guest-list. It took some time for her to respond to my query, and she did not have a clear answer. Then I went on to explain to her the meaning of untouchability.

Before I proceeded, I made it clear that I was not questioning her anti-varna/caste credentials; but untouchability is such a doctrine that it does not fully liberate even a most rational, most emancipated, forward-looking person from practising it, howsoever unconsciously. I said, contrary to the popular perception that untouchability is a 'social evil', it is in essence a doctrine of *exclusion*. I pointed out, that the basic dividing line in Indian society is between those who are part of the chaturvarna order, and those who are excluded from it—the untouchables and adivasis. Only recently, say since the arrival of the British, did the dalits get some idea of what was within that order. The evolution of India into a republic in 1950 was a moment of rupture, where the state was directed to end that age-old system of exclusion, and reconstruct society along democratic lines. Bound by that verdict of the Constitution, the state has given some space in institutions under its direct control. But society, by and large, has been refusing to internalize that verdict to the hilt, and therefore dalits remain excluded from institutions outside the command of the state.

I continued offering many examples. I pointed out the implications of such exclusion. I said, make a list of one hundred leading writers/editors/anchors/artists who are nationally known, including the editor of *The Pioneer*, and examine if any one of them ever had a chance of dining with an untouchable family, in an informal/non-official occasion, though, all of them, I insist, will be genuinely against the 'evil' of untouchability? I continued, if there is not a single dalit who is an editor of a national daily, an anchor on TV channels, or a member of FICCI [Federation of Indian Chambers of Commerce and Industry] or CII [Confederation of Indian Industry], it is not by incident, but by virtue of the doctrine of untouchability. This creates the material conditions and spins a web, which in turn conditions the existential condition of the varna members to the extent that howsoever consciously they wish to fight the 'evil', they remain prisoners of this doctrine all their life.

Dalit Diary may not end that exclusion in the foreseeable future; it may have no potential to revolutionize the minds of varna members, whom the chaturvarna order does not suffocate, and who have for centuries enjoyed the taste of gutter-culture, and it may never convert all dalit thinkers into writers, but it has definitely opened a new chapter in Indian journalism. Its first anniversary also enabled some varna members to wash their sins, although only partially. Hats off to *The Pioneer* family, and its editor, Chandan Mitra.

The Pioneer, 9 April 2000

LOVE-LINES IN THE TIMES OF CHATURVARNA

Meera Bai, the great sixteenth-century bhakti poetess, was poisoned twice. First, by her in-laws outraged by the fact that a rajput woman had dared to join the sangati and sing bhajans in public. The second instance was prompted by a totally different reason. The poetess, inspired by the genius of the great dalit saint, Ravidas, had declared him her guru. Her affection, a purely intellectual/spiritual affair, was disliked by the rajput clan. Meera lived during the fifteenth–sixteenth centuries. Around the same period, Europe had just entered the era of Enlightenment.

But about five hundred years later, when people can make love in cyberspace, how do we explain the painful story of Hardoi, close to the capital city Lucknow, where a number of internet cafés are in operation? A dalit boy from Hardoi and a rajput girl fell in love, think-ing 'love is blind'. Their imagination transcended the social ghettoes they were born in, and their dreams touched newer heights when they decided to script a new world for themselves. What they prob-ably did not realize was that civil society, like a radar, was watching their flight.

The might of the rajput fraternity fell on the couple, and the boy and three members of his family had to pay the price with their lives. But this is not the first occasion when a dalit tried to redefine love and suffered for it. You may recollect the gory event of 1992 in Mathura district. A dalit boy and a jat girl entered a similar union. The jat pan-chayat swung into action and delivered its verdict. In broad daylight, in the presence of a crowd, it hanged the couple to death.

A cursory reading of the Manu-dharma shastra would unfold the secrets of the chaturvarna order. According to the varna laws, occupation and marriage are the two foundations on which the social order stands. No one is allowed to marry outside his or her varna or caste and no one is allowed a change of occupation. Any defiance of these twin laws would attract heavy penalties, including death. Society, even after the enactment of the Indian Penal Code, religiously follows these codes in ways that are sometimes too subtle.

The district administration had described the Hardoi murders as a result of a dispute between two families. On the face of it, this explanation seems convincing as the boy and the girl belong to two different families. But it is also a fact that both the boy and the girl belong to two different communities—from within and without the chaturvarna order. One wonders had the boy belonged to a rajput community, or any community belonging to the walled confines of the varna order, would there still have been such murders? Love has its limitations.

It has to materialize within the boundaries of the social group lovers are born in. Any defiance of the Manu-dharma shastra attracts penalties. But some would argue that this rigidity is essentially a countryside phenomenon, and the urban, enlightened sections have made a decisive departure from it. Often confronted by such opinions, I introspected. I made a list of two-dozen friends who, after a pronged experimentation with love, had decided to be life-partners. Since most of them are, I am sure, committed critics of the chaturvarna order, I had to conduct the exercise under utmost secrecy. The results were appalling if not totally outrageous.

I still wonder why most of my brahmin friends happen to fall in love only with brahmin girls and vice versa. Similarly, most of my kayastha friends fell in love with kayasthas, and the same holds true of other friends belonging to other communities of the varna order. Some took the brave step of loving and marrying outside their religions, but a close scrutiny shows that while they broke the religion barriers, they singularly failed to break the varna/caste barriers.

That means lovers have a love-line, below which neither love nor marriage can take place. What a society this is, where love has been redefined to the narrowest compass with people who perpetuate it and willingly subject themselves to social censure.

The Pioneer, 14 May 2000

M.M. VINODINI

M.M. Vinodini (1969–) is a dalit feminist writer and scholar from Andhra Pradesh. Her work focuses on reading feminist questions in the dalit context. Born into a family of Dalit Christians, she does not lay claim to the Left lineage that most Telugu dalit writers have. Her stories have been published in collections such as Katha *(2009) and* Katha Varshika *(2010). She is an assistant professor at Yogi Vemana University, Kadapa.*

THE PARABLE OF THE LOST DAUGHTER: LUKE 15; 11–32 [1]

"Didn't you say they were brahmins! Will they let us into their home, dear?"

"I don't know about you ... but they will certainly let *me* come in," said Suvarthavani, smiling as she parted her hair looking into the mirror.

Those were soft baby feet that kicked him on the chest, but they really hurt all the same. But Paladasu collected himself thinking—

It was true; he didn't even have proper clothes to wear. Carpentry in the day and plying the rickshaw at night till the second shows of cinema were over meant that he was dirty and unkempt all the time. His feet were always covered in dust—in fact, he had not known foot-wear since the time he was born. But his daughter—no one would believe that she was his girl—she was so pretty!

He continued, "Listen dear, you know this, I mean, we are lower caste..."

"Father, they are not at all like that. They don't care about caste or religion. My friend's father has written many books saying that

---

[1] This is a reference to the parable of the lost son/the prodigal son, which Vinodini uses to write about a 'lost' dalit girl.

all human beings are equal. I have been to their house several times when I was in Rajahmundry. I moved freely in the entire house. My friend even took me into their kitchen."

"Oh! In that case, you can go. Set out now and keep safe," he said.

"Where the hell are you? Why don't you say something," he yelled for his wife as he hauled the suitcase onto his shoulder. "I will go to the railway station to help our daughter catch the train. If Devasahayam comes, ask him to wait for me," and then turning to his daughter, said, "Let's go now."

"Oh Father! Let that be. Put that suitcase down. Why should you come all the way to the station? Call another rickshaw. I will go myself."

"No. How will you carry all this weight, dear? Let me come with you."

"No! Listen to me, there's no need. Didn't you say you had some work … and you said uncle Devasahayam was coming too?"

Paladasu knew his daughter wasn't going to let him come to the station. He went out to fetch another rickshaw.

Krupamma closed the steel tiffin box and wiped it with her sari. "Egg curry, dear," she said. "Today is Thursday, so I bought meat. But it's no use! I know you won't eat it!" She put the box in a polythene bag and handed it to her daughter.

"Ma, it doesn't agree with me anymore. Why else won't I eat it?"

Zacharaiah was taking out the steaming hot thigh bone from the stove. He put it in a vessel and sat himself down before the stone mortar. He said, "You ate it for more than twenty years! Why won't it agree with you now? You're just putting on airs. You stopped eating not because you don't like it anymore, but just so that you can tell your friends that you don't eat beef." Zachariah was Suvarthavani's younger brother. He was named Zachariah because he was short just like the Zachariah in the Bible.

He gripped the hot bone, which was the size of his forearm, firmly in his palm. He beat it hard against the mortar, quickly picked up the juicy marrow that slipped out and put it into his mouth. Savouring it slowly, he turned to his sister and said, "Come Sunday and you would start pestering Mother, 'Mother, please get liver, also get blood. Don't come back without the thigh bone. And Ma, cook it with gongura.' You would hardly wait for the curry to be cooked, the vessel would still be on the stove and you'd be picking out the pieces and eating them up. But now just because you're into higher studies, you stopped eating." He continued teasingly, "I know that even now your mouth waters for this."

"Yes, I stopped eating so that you can eat your fill," she spat out the words angrily. But it was not simply anger; she was in fact irked that her brother had brought this up for discussion.

"Don't pay attention to him, dear. And write to us as soon as you reach," her mother said, as if she was a small girl. Actually, her mother wanted to stroke her daughter's back as she said this, but the deep dark lines that had formed on her palms, and her finger nails filled with the ash she used to scrub vessels in different houses, stopped her from doing so.

"Ok, I will write. But look at your sari! Why have you hitched it up so high? Pull it down. How many times have I said to you, 'Comb your hair as soon as you wake up...?'"

Before Suvarthavani could finish her sentence, Zachariah laughing aloud, took over and began imitating her, "...and to use some face powder, wear ironed clothes, cook on the gas stove, watch TV..."

By this time, all the marrow in the bone had oozed out. He placed the bone on the edge of the mortar, and closed one end with his palm. And on the other end, which was dark brown, he hit slowly but firmly. The bone broke into many pieces. He chewed on each piece like he would chew a sugarcane piece and spat out the leftovers. Every now and then he threw a piece to the dog. Watching her brother infuriated Suvarthavani. "Chi! I don't want to talk to you!" Suvarthavani went out and sat in the rickshaw that Paladasu had just fetched for her.

"Travel safely, daughter," Krupamma said as she pulled down the sari that she had hitched almost above her knees. Once again, she pleaded as if she was speaking to a little girl.

Suvarthavani had always occupied a special place in that house.

She was intelligent and very good at her studies. She was good-looking too. Although they lived in a small village near Guntur, Krupamma and Paladasu decided that they would help her study as much as she wanted to. They wanted their daughter to have a life that was unlike theirs. They wanted her to be happy and respected, and they believed that education alone helped a person achieve these.

Suvarthavani liked Telugu literature and loved the river Godavari immensely. But it was not for these reasons that she did her M.A. in Rajahmundry; it was solely because of the good marks she scored that she was able to join college there. Suvarthavani loved her classmate Gayatri just as much as she loved literature and the Godavari. Because he wrote stories and novels, she loved Gayatri's father, Piratla Subramaniam. And because Gayatri's mother, Kameswaramma, always looked serene and calm like the August Godavari, Suvarthavani loved her too.

When Gayatri invited her home for the first time, Suvarthavani felt a strange anxiety and excitement. She had never ever visited a brahmin home until then. In fact, she had never had brahmin friends before. She visited yanadi homes while she was in elementary school, and later, during her high school and B.A. years, she had visited Christian homes. She had even gone to the homes of Hindus belonging to other castes, but this was the first time that she was going to a brahmin house.

They had to walk a few paces from the bus stop to reach Gayatri's house. On the way, they passed a temple.

Gayatri paused near the temple, looked at Suvarthavani's face, and said, "How do I take you home? Your face looks bare!"

"Just a minute," she said, as she reached for a red Reynolds pen in her handbag.

Gayatri held her face and said, "Don't move," as she tried to shape a red dot on Suvarthavani's forehead. The pen wasn't working. "This isn't working well. Come here." She led Suvarthavani into the temple. It was an Anjaneya Swamy temple. "You aren't having your periods, are you?" she asked, looking suspiciously.

"No," mumbled Suvarthavani.

Gayatri took the vermilion in the temple and applied it to her forehead. Suvarthavani felt lost, she was wearing a bottu for the first time in her life. She had never worn one even for fun.

"Oh! You look so beautiful! You look transformed. A bottu really enhances a woman's beauty. Your face is glowing now."

Kameswaramma was all praise for Suvarthavani. "Never mind her caste. She is a lovely girl. She speaks so clearly, such chaste pronunciation! Gayatri, you should learn the language from her."

That day, everything in their house appeared to her in a haze. Even Gayatri's mother, father, brother, everyone was in a blur. Suvarthavani went to Gayatri's house again a few times. They all seemed to add an extra 'h' to every word they uttered. And without realizing it, she too would speak in the same way while she was in their house. Later, she would do many things 'unknowingly'. For example, saying 'Vani', instead of 'Suvarthavani' when asked for her name; writing 'S. Vani' when she had to write it; listening to the classical poetry that some lecturers belted out even when all her classmates had fled the class and even if she had the most splitting of headaches. Borrowing heavy and dusty Sanskrit tomes from the library that no one ever bothered to even glance at ... attending locally held events of traditional classical literature and actually waiting till the very end!

Whenever she went to the canteen or the mess, she'd be very particular about 'used' plates, and spilt or left-over food on the tables, and fuss about clean hands and unclean hands. She would be more conscious and worried about these things than everyone else. Even when her friends took food from each other's tiffin boxes with their bare hands, she would look around for a spoon or ladle. She would hide details of the food they cooked and ate at home and instead describe how her mother made brinjal curry, sambhar and coconut-and-lentil chutney, like the food she had seen her friends bring for lunch. In addition to these, she had picked up other significant habits like, 'bunking church, wearing a red thread around her wrist like she had seen many Hindus do, and wearing a bottu whenever she visited Gayatri's house.'

Gayatri's sister was pregnant and there was a function arranged to celebrate this. This was another chance for Suvarthavani to visit Gayatri's house. Going there was always a pleasant and pleasurable experience for her. She felt as if she was throwing away into the rubbish heap her crude, old and worn-out footwear made with cow leather, and was slipping effortlessly into a pair of delicate and comfortable fine sandals made of leaves.

Gayatri had warned Suvarthavani a week in advance that she could come to the function only if her grandmother or Uncle Bachi did not attend. Grandma was so particular about their traditions that she was known to even wash fire in order to purify it! And Uncle Bachi was not only equally traditional but, in addition, was also interested in preparing the horoscopes of unwed young girls to examine their marriage prospects. Indeed, if Uncle Bachi were to ask her birth star and the exact time she was born at, and her zodiac sign and blah, blah, blah, what would she tell him? And if he discovered her caste in the process, Gayatri would surely be reprimanded for bringing her there. So, Suvarthavani was fervently hoping they wouldn't come, and they didn't!

Many people who saw her at the function quickly got down to match-making. But when they came to know about Suvarthavani's caste, they were taken aback wondering, "Are there such lovely girls among the harijans!" On these occasions when Gayatri had to reveal her friend's caste, both she and Suvarthavani felt very uncomfortable. Gayatri would whisper the caste name furtively, as if she was uttering something unspeakable. And Suvarthavani looked guiltily at people, like a thief who had been caught in the act. On hearing the caste name, some consoled her saying, "We thought she was a kamma or a reddy, doesn't look like a harijan girl at all!" Not only did Suvarthavani feel consoled by such remarks, she also felt proud. Her house, her neighbourhood and her own people all looked very small now! Suvarthavani took huge leaps to move as far away as she could from them to reach the other side.

Gayatri was applying turmeric to the feet of all the women assembled at the function. Suvarthavani too put out her feet for the turmeric. But Gayatri said quickly, "I shouldn't touch your feet, Vani.

Brahmins shouldn't touch the feet of harijans." Hurt, Suvarthavani quickly withdrew her feet. Gayatri patiently applied turmeric to all kinds of feet—feet sore from being constantly wet; feet that were coarse with cracked heels and rough skin; feet that were so dry that their skin was peeling away; feet that were dusty and dirty with toe nails that were encrusted with mud—she used her delicate soft hands to rub turmeric on all of them. But she did not touch Suvarthavani's feet. But Suvarthavani was content just to be there at the gathering. But she didn't like the sight of her own pale feet amidst all those bright yellow feet. So, she took some turmeric and rubbed it on her feet herself.

The small joys and proud moments that she gathered on such occasions turned into dislike, anger and frustration whenever she went home for the holidays. She hated the fact that her own parents looked nothing like Gayatri's parents. She began to dislike the way they spoke, their habits, their work, everything annoyed her now. Sometimes, she just found it all quite despicable. She would constantly talk to them in an irritated and impatient tone. She found fault with everything they did. Soon, they got used to her behaviour.

After completing her M.A., Gayatri got married and left for the United States. Her father, Piratla Subramaniam, had retired and moved to Hyderabad, built a house and settled down there. Suvarthavani was working part-time in the Ambedkar Open University and was also doing her research. She came home for the vacation. When she received a call to attend the spot valuation at the university in Hyderabad, she set out for the city.

*

"The rain is quite foolish! It's okay for it to be pouring hard in the village, why should it rain here in this big city." Suvarthavani got off the train at Secunderabad station cursing the downpour. She gave Subramaniam's address to the auto driver and got in.

On the way, she began thinking of Gayatri's family. She knew that Gayatri's parents and her elder sister and brother-in-law, both of whom worked in Hyderabad, lived in the house together. The sister had rented one part of the house and the parents lived in the other. The auto was getting drenched in the rain as it sped along the Tankbund. The road shone like a river of black tar. With her head bent slightly, Suvarthavani was watching the statues lined along the bund side. Jashuva! He stood there proud and tall with a glowing self-respect despite the showers of humiliation he had endured. All of a sudden, she remembered something. She removed the chain she was wearing around her neck and took off the pendant that was hanging from it. She wore the chain again. She opened her palm and looked at the pendant—it was a cross. Smiling, she said, "Sorry, Jesus," and threw it into one corner of her handbag. She took out a small packet of sticker-bottus and stuck a bottu on her forehead. Ah! She felt relieved now. The auto drove past Ambedkar standing at the end of Tankbund.

It was easy enough to find the address. It was a newly constructed house. The morning air was filled with the smell of incense.

"It's for a week, Father... Starting today until the twenty-second."

"Don't they provide accommodation there?" Subramaniam asked sharply.

"No, Father, most people are renting rooms in a lodge, four to five in one room. Even women are forced to do it. But I came here," she said smiling. She got up to put away her coffee cup in the kitchen sink. "Wait," said Kameswaramma. "We've just finished the puja for the day, so it is better if you don't enter the kitchen and the puja room." Suvarthavani left the cup in a corner of the living room.

Suvarthavani had always wanted to cement the friendship she had with Gayatri. As part of this effort, she behaved as if Gayatri's parents and Gayatri's house were her own. She would address Gayatri's sister and bother-in-law as 'Sister' and 'Brother-in-law'. She would call Gayatri's parents 'Mother' and 'Father'. She would refer to Gayatri's house as 'our house'. When she spoke about her own family, she simply said Mother, Father or Brother. However, Gayatri always said, 'my mother', 'my father' and 'your mother' and 'your father', always specifying whom she was referring to.

Even now, Suvarthavani believed strongly that she was close enough to the family to come and stay in their house for the week although Gayatri was no longer there. Rather, she hoped that she was close enough to do so. Indeed, she also hoped in one corner of her mind that they would gift her a sari when it was time to leave, just like they did whenever close relatives visited.

She spoke to Kameswaramma affectionately and enquired about each and every one of their family members and relatives and even all their children by name. Many of them she had never even met, but she had heard of them through Gayatri. Kameswaramma didn't ask her in turn about the welfare of her family. In fact, she didn't even know anything about Suvarthavani's family, she didn't know about her parents or her siblings. Even Gayatri had never cared to ask.

*

Suvarthavani had to go daily to the university in Jubilee Hills by bus and auto. In the evenings she had to visit bookshops and libraries. So it was quite late by the time she came back each day. The family usually finished their dinner by that time and left hers in a plate in her room. They had given her the small room that connected the front portion where Subramaniam and Kameswaramma lived with the rear portion of the house where Gayatri's sister lived with her husband. Suvarthavani was really pleased that they had given her that room because it contained all the bookshelves. One half of a book-shelf consisted of books that Subramaniam himself had authored. Oppressed castes, exploited classes, the poor and the needy, lonely women, prostitutes—these were his subjects. Many of his stories and plays featured young, handsome eligible men from upper castes mar-rying women from such classes and castes. She read these each day before going to bed. She was very eager to discuss them at length with Subramaniam. But he always answered her in the driest of tones. He was always nagging his wife or scolding someone or the other loudly over the phone. Apart from the one or two sentences he spoke with her on the day she arrived, he did not speak to her again.

From the third day of her stay, Suvarthavani began to get very anxious. It was that time of the month—she would get her periods any day now. Should she tell them at all? If she did, should she tell Mother or Sister? Would she also have to sit separately in that small space near the bathroom without touching the rest of them, like Gayatri's sister did recently? Would she have to wash her own plate and glass and leave it there too? If she did this, the men of the house too would come to know that she was having her periods! That would be quite shameful. Maybe, she shouldn't tell any of them ... maybe she should just keep it a secret. But how to dispose of the used napkin? Should she just wrap it up and put it away in her suitcase along with the used clothes? Or put it in her handbag and throw it away once she got out of the house? But if she kept this a secret, would it not amount to cheating these people? Would it not be an insult to their traditions? All this wouldn't have mattered in her house, but here... Thankfully, the day of her departure arrived, but her periods hadn't. Suvarthavani was relieved. Today was her last day here.

That evening as she walked back from the bus stop earlier than usual, she met Gayatri's brother-in-law on the way. He stopped his scooter and offered her a lift. "Aren't you early today?" he asked.

She hesitated slightly before getting onto the vehicle. "I didn't have any extra work today," she replied, smiling shyly.

"Hold me tight ... the roads are really bad." He seemed to be aiming for all the ditches in the road and was repeatedly applying the brakes. Suvarthavani had been puzzled and irked by his behaviour from the very start. He acted too familiar. He would come in every morning and wish her. He would knock on the bathroom door several times while she was bathing to ask her if she was done. If she was holding their baby, he would touch her breasts lightly while taking the child from her. Sometimes he would come into her room after eleven in the night when everyone else was asleep and ask her to come watch TV with him. During the day, he always talked of tradition and puja and so on. Gayatri had always talked about how her brother-in-law greatly respected traditions. But his behaviour belied this all the time.

"Why are you so quiet? Do you watch films?" he asked her.

"Sometimes."

"English films?"

"I've recently started watching some."

"Have you seen this? He pointed to a wall poster."

It was an obscene poster depicting a man and woman who were half-naked embracing each other. She felt revolted. She also felt wounded and insulted by his gesture.

When she didn't answer, he turned back and grinned, "Come on... Haven't you seen it?"

"No."

"Oh, you haven't? You know we should learn to enjoy life! You are Christian. You are not a traditional girl! What's there to stop you? My wife and Gayatri ... they are always talking of tradition, morality, chastity and other such nonsensical stuff. They carry such notions in their heads. They are too orthodox. We cannot change them. But you are free. You don't need to carry those burdens. You can enjoy life freely. So why should you stick to our traditions?"

"If you don't mind, let me ask you something ... come, let's talk over coffee," he said as he stopped near a café and led her in. She walked behind him reluctantly. She could see the half-hidden brahmin lock in his 'modern' crop of hair. He also wore a tiny vermilion dot on his forehead and many a sacred thread adorned his wrist.

He continued as he sipped a cool drink: "Science has developed so much nowadays. You don't need to be afraid of anything. I am friendly with many Christian girls. You know what it means to be friends, right?" He winked as he said this.

"There are so many things I like about Christian girls. They wear modern clothes. They don't care whether it is a man or woman, they ride on bikes. They are willing to come along wherever you wish to go—a movie, a park, anywhere. They really know how to use their freedom. They don't hesitate to sit close to you or to shake hands. They don't propose such sentimental nonsense as marriage. And what's more, you can hug them and roll around and kiss them just as you please, there's no danger of spoiling the bottu on their foreheads!" He laughed out loudly.

Suvarthavani felt her mouth go dry. She felt as if the divider from her school geometry box was stretched straight to pierce both her palms at once. Such contempt for her caste and her community! How could he talk so cheaply? He, who always seemed so preoccupied by pujas and traditions!

"Why are you staring at me like that? Perhaps you don't know this. In the city 'the women from your community' are like this. But why speak only of the city! The village women are no less. As you know, all the men from the big houses use the women from the harijanwada. Oh! It's so thrilling to take these women in the sugarcane fields or amidst the maize fields. But you know in the village, there is always the danger of someone getting pregnant. Whereas here, you know there have been such advances in science, we don't need to worry about such things."

She felt as if the wounds in her palms were now bleeding slowly. She stood up abruptly and walked out of the café silently. He walked behind her.

She came home and went straight into the bathroom and washed her face. But she didn't feel any better. She washed her hair and her whole body with cold water. The more she thought about all the things he had said about the women from her caste and community, the more a fierce agony filled her. It was as if a sharp knife dug deep into her body and cut her open. She couldn't eat that night. She went into her room, turned off the light and lay down on the bed.

It was September and the Hyderabad cold was already severe. The cold had caused all the wooden doors to expand—it was hard to close any of them properly. The family was worried about a possible burglary. So, the carpenters had been called in that day. They shaved off the extra wood and fitted in new bolts and locks for all the doors. This took all day and it was nine by the time Kameswaramma checked all the doors and paid the carpenters before sending them away. Subramaniam called around ten to say that he would be home in an hour and a half.

Suvarthavani couldn't sleep. She didn't feel like reading anything either. Every word that Brother-in-law had said in the café echoed in her head and she felt that each of the things he said about Christian girls was aimed at her. She had such respect for their culture and traditions, but they had nothing but hatred and contempt for her caste and her people. Her head was spinning. "They really think that we were unworthy of any regard or respect—they have such disdain for us." And she had shared those ideas! She was so anxious to speak, dress and behave like them. She had even taken to wearing a bottu just like Hindu girls, so that she would be seen as one of them. But despite all this, to them she was still a harijan girl, a Christian girl!

She began to think of the number of times she was humiliated and insulted because of her caste. She thought of the time Gayatri placed a bottu on her forehead without even asking her. She thought of the time when Gayatri avoided rubbing turmeric on her feet alone in that large gathering of women. It didn't matter that she was her friend. She was a harijan and therefore untouchable. Why did she ever think that their customs and their language were respectable? Why could she not respect her own language and culture?

She heard the sound of the scooter... Subramaniam must have come home. Kameswaramma opened the door for him. Suvarthavani looked at the time. It was half-past midnight. After about five minutes, she heard him shouting loudly. "You filthy bitch! What have you been doing all day ... displaying your body to those low-caste bastards? You rotten old whore, why was the bolt not fitted on the main gate? Did you sleep with those bastards that you let them off with only half the work done! You mala bitch ... you madiga bitch ... you act just like those low caste bitches. You've picked up all their habits ... you Christian bitch, why don't you hook up with that bastard of a carpenter ... those mala madiga buggers." He went on and on. There was no shutting him up.

Suvarthavani was shocked to hear him abuse his wife using such foul language. Abusive language was not new to her. It was common enough in her own family and in her community. But it blended seamlessly into their life and language. Those terms were used to express love, affection and intimacy. They were also used to express anger and rage. However, this kind of hatred and contempt was not common. In fact, she had never seen such repulsive and humiliating language used between two people who were bound by ties of love and marriage.

Moreover, she couldn't understand what link there was between the abuses Subramaniam hurled at Kameswaramma and her negligible error of overlooking a bolt. She hadn't ever imagined that Subramaniam could speak such language. She looked at the bookshelf and the rows of books he had written. There was nothing in common between the lofty words spoken by the protagonists of those books and the abuses that he used just now. And it was not just his wife that he abused. He had abused her too! He abused her caste, her religion, and the women of her community, and the men of her community.

Suvarthavani was not sure if it was the divider or the knife now which pierced her wildly and indiscriminately ... up, down, here, there ... her body was being carved into pieces. The pain from these invisible wounds began to hurt her immensely. It kept her awake all night. She remembered her home. Her heart was filled with agony. The dim haze that had eclipsed her mother and father, her brother, her house, her neighbourhood was all gone! They stood in a clear light now, waiting for her.

Finally it dawned on her. Suvarthavani woke up and bathed. It was the day of her departure. She put together all her things. She opened her purse and took out the little Jesus pendant and wore it. She left her forehead clear and bare. She threw the bottu packet into the dustbin, took her suitcase and stepped out into the living room.

The whole family was sitting there. She told them that it was the last day of work and that she was going to leave straight from the university. "Goodbye," said Suvarthavani and proceeded to wear her sandals without waiting for a response.

Kameswaramma said, "Girl, you seem to have forgotten your bottu."

"No, Mother. I haven't forgotten. I am a Christian girl. I am a dalit girl." She smiled and stepped out of the house as if there was nothing more to be said.

Translated from Telugu by Uma Bhrugubanda

S. JOSEPH

S. Joseph (1965–) was born into a communist artisanal family in Kerala. He has observed both the Naxalite movement and the dalit movement from a distance, and though he has lent his support to certain causes, feels that poetry ought not to be gripped by a movement. In his view, his poetry is about all people outside the mainstream, and he invokes hitherto unseen landscapes and objects in his writing. Joseph has published several books, including Karutha Kallu *(Black Stone, 2000) his first, and* Identity Card *(2006).*

IDENTITY CARD

In my student days
a girl came laughing

Our hands met mixing
her rice and fish curry

On a bench we became
a Hindu–Christian family

I whiled away my time
reading Neruda's poetry;
and meanwhile I misplaced
my Identity Card.

She said,
returning my card:
'the account of your stipend
is entered there in red.'

These days I never look at
a boy and a girl lost in themselves.
They will part after a while.

I won't be surprised even if they unite.
Their Identity Cards
won't have markings in red.

MY SISTER'S BIBLE

These are what my sister's Bible has:
a ration-book come loose,
a loan application form,
a card from the cut-throat moneylender,
the notices of feasts
in the church and the temple,
a photograph of my brother's child,
a paper that says how to knit a baby-cap,
a hundred-rupee note,
an SSLC Book.
These are what my sister's Bible doesn't have:
preface,
the Old Testament and the New,
maps,
the red cover.

Translated from Malayalam by K. Satchidanandan

FURTHER READING: A SELECT LIST

Bagul, Baburao. "Dalit Literature is but Human Literature." In *Poisoned Bread: Translations from Modern Marathi Dalit Literature*. Edited by Arjun Dangle, 271–89. Hyderabad: Orient Longman, 1992. [essay]

Bama, *Karukku*. Trans. Lakshmi Holmström. Chennai: Macmillan, 2000. 2nd edn., New Delhi: Oxford University Press, 2012. [autobiography]

Baxi, Upendra. "Emancipation as Justice: Babasaheb Ambedkar's Legacy and Vision." In *Ambedkar and Social Justice*. Vol. 1, New Delhi: Publications Division, Government of India, 1995, 13–34. Also in *Crisis and Change in Contemporary India*, edited by Upendra Baxi and Bhikhu Parekh, 122–49. New Delhi: Sage, 1995. [essay]

Chentharassery, T.H.P. *Kerala Charithrathile Avaganikkappetta Edukal* (The Ignored Aspects of Kerala History). Thiruvananthapuram: Prabath Book House, 1970. [History]

Deshpande, G.P. "Of Hope and Melancholy: Reading Jotirao Phule in Our Times." In *Selected Writings of Jotirao Phule*, edited by G.P. Deshpande, 1–21. New Delhi: LeftWord, 2002. [essay]

Dangle, Arjun. "Dalit Literature: Past, Present, Future." In *Poisoned Bread: Translations from Modern Marathi Dalit Literature*, edited by Arjun Dangle, 234–66. Hyderabad: Orient Longman, 1992. [essay]

Guru, Gopal. "The Politics of Naming." *Seminar* 471 (November 1998): 14–18. [essay, theory]

Kalekuri Prasad. "The Dalit Movement and the Dalit Literary Movement." In *Steel Nibs are Sprouting: New Dalit Writing from South India, Dossier 2: Kannada and Telugu*, edited by K. Satyanarayana and Susie Tharu, 604–21. New Delhi: HarperCollins, 2013. [essay, theory]

Kapikkad, Sunny M. "Kerala Model: A Dalit Critique." In *No Alphabet in Sight: New Dalit Writing from South India, Dossier 1: Tamil and Malayalam*, edited by K. Satyanarayana and Susie Tharu, 464–74. New Delhi: Penguin. [essay, political analysis]

Mohan, Sanal. "Narrativising the History of Slave Suffering." In *No Alphabet in Sight: New Dalit Writing from South India, Dossier 1: Ta-*

mil and Malayalam, edited by K. Satyanarayana and Susie Tharu, 535–55. New Delhi: Penguin. [history, cultural analysis]

Moon, Vasant. *Growing Up Untouchable in India*, translated by Gail Omvedt. New Delhi: Vistaar, 2000. [autobiography]

Nagaraj, D.R. "Between Social Rage and Spiritual Quest: Notes on Dalit Writing in Kannada." In *The Flaming Feet and other Essays: The Dalit Movement in India*, edited by Prithvi Datta Chandra Shobhi, , 218–22. New Delhi: Permanent Black, 2010. [essay]

Natarajan, Srividya and Aparajita Ninan. *A Gardener in the Wasteland: Jotiba Phule's Fight for Liberty*. New Delhi: Navayana, 2011. [graphic novel, history]

Omvedt, Gail. "The Turning Point, 1930–36: Ambedkar, Gandhi, the Marxists." In *Dalits and Democratic Revolution: Dr Ambedkar and the Dalit Movement in Colonial India*. New Delhi: Sage Publications, 1994, 161–89. [historical analysis]

Pandian, M.S.S. "Stepping Outside History? New Dalit writings from Tamilnadu." In *Wages of Freedom*, edited by Partha Chatterjee. New Delhi: Oxford University Press, 1998, 293–309. [essay].

Puttaiah, B.M. "Does Dalit literature Need Poetics?" in *Steel Nibs are Sprouting: New Dalit Writing from South India, Dossier 2: Kannada and Telugu*. New Delhi: HarperCollins, 2013, 350–68. [essay, theory]

Rege, Sharmila. "Debating the Consumption of Dalit Autobiographies." *Writing caste/Writing Gender: Narrating Dalit Women's Testimonios*. New Delhi: Zubaan, 2006, 9–92. [criticism, theory]

Satyanarayana, K., and Susie Tharu. "Introduction." *No Alphabet in Sight: New Dalit Writing from South India, Dossier 1: Tamil and Malayalam*, edited by Satyanarayana and Tharu. New Delhi: Penguin, 2011, 1–72. [background material, criticism]

———. "Introduction." *From Those Stubs, Steel Nibs are Sprouting: New Dalit Writing from South India, Dossier 2: Kannada and Telugu*, edited by Satyanarayana and Tharu. New Delhi: HarperCollins, 2013, 1–56. [background material, criticism]

Gogu Shyamala, *Father May Be an Elephant and Mother only a Small Basket, But...*. New Delhi: Navayana, 2012. [fiction]

from Tamil by Meena Kandasamy; K. Satyanarayana and Susie Tharu, "A Brief Introduction to Kerala Dalit Literature"; Mathivannan, "On *Scavenger's Son*", translated from Tamil by Theodore Baskaran; Raghavan Atholi, "Poet with a Forest Fire Inside", translated from Malayalam by Jayasree Kalathil; T.M Yesudasan, excerpts from "Towards a Prologue to Dalit Studies", translated from Malayalam by the author; S. Joseph, "Identity Card", "My Sister's Bible", translated from Malayalam by K. Satchidanandan—all from *No Alphabet in Sight: New Dalit Writing from South India, Dossier 1: Tamil and Malayalam*, edited by K. Satyanarayana and Susie Tharu, published by Penguin Books India, New Delhi, 2011.

Siddalingaiah, "Thousands of Rivers", "The Dalits are Here", translated from Kannada by M. Madhava Prasad; Devanoora Mahadeva, "Tar Comes", translated from Kannada by Manu Shetty and A.K. Ramanujan; H. Govindaiah, "A Letter to Father", translated from Kannada by Ankur Betageri; B. Krishnappa, "Dalit Literature", translated from Kannada by Maithreyi M.R.; Challapalli Swaroopa Rani, "Water", translated from Telugu by Uma Bhrugubanda; M.M. Vinodini, "The Parable of the Lost Daughter", translated from Telugu by Uma Bhrugubanda—all from *From Those Stubs, Steel Nibs are Sprouting: New Dalit Writing from South India, Dossier 2: Kannada and Telugu*, edited by K. Satyanarayana and Susie Tharu, published by HarperCollins Publishers India, New Delhi, 2013.

OTHER NAVAYANA TITLES

A Word With You, World: The Autobiography of a Poet
Siddalingaiah
tr. S.R. Ramakrishna
Autobiography | Paperback | 302 pages | Rs 395

Unclaimed Terrain
Ajay Navaria
tr. Laura Brueck
Fiction | Hardback | 200 pages | Rs 295

Father May Be an Elephant and Mother Only a Small Basket, But...
Gogu Shyamala
tr. from Telugu
Fiction | Hardback | 263 pages | Rs 350

In the Tiger's Shadow: The Autobiography of an Ambedkarite
Namdeo Nimgade
Autobiography | Paperback | 290 pages | Rs 350

A Current of Blood
Namdeo Dhasal
tr. Dilip Chitre
Poetry | Paperback | 120 pages | Rs 180

Give Us This Day a Feast of Flesh
N.D. Rajkumar
tr. Anushiya Ramaswamy
Poetry | Paperback | 110 pages | Rs 180

In Pursuit of Ambedkar: A Memoir
Bhagwan Das (with DVD of documentary feature)
Autobiography | Paperback | 86 pages | Rs 175

Ambedkar's World: The Making of Babasaheb and the Dalit Movement
Eleanor Zelliot
Paperback | 304 pages | Rs 295

Bhimayana: Experiences of Untouchability
art: Durgabai Vyam, Subhash Vyam
text: Srividya Natarajan, S. Anand
Graphic novel in colour | Paperback | 108 pages | Rs 395